"This message mu...

"Mark Cahill has become the favorite speaker at our Summit camps and conferences, but it's not because his teaching is fascinating (it is). Nor is it because his approach to evangelism eliminates fear and inspires confidence (it does). Mark is top-notch because he's the real deal. He walks the talk. He has challenged me personally to share my faith in all I do, all the time. I've accepted the challenge and hope you will too."

>JEFF MYERS, PH.D.
>Director, The Summit
>Asst. Prof. of Communication Arts, Bryan College

"Mark Cahill is one of the most zealous and passionate Christians I know. He reminds me of what the early Christians must have been like as they spread this good news of the Gospel. Mark doesn't fit in the conventional, comfortable church because he is not conventional, and he is not comfortable. Praise the Lord. Perhaps the best part is that his zeal is contagious and I have witnessed its effect in many settings. Everyone is challenged; many are never the same again."

>SHERRI MCCREADY
>Director, Choice Lifestyle Ministries

"In my many years as a faculty member at Summit Ministries, Mark Cahill more than any other speaker was able to motivate and capture the students' hearts for a life of evangelism. His contagious excitement about reaching the lost for Christ will undoubtedly 'infect' you as you read this book, and you will experience a new vigor for sharing the Gospel of Jesus Christ."

>DR. JOBE MARTIN
>President, Biblical Discipleship Ministries
>Rockwall, Texas

"Mark Cahill had a stunning impact on our student body. His passion for evangelism and his ability to communicate effective principles is unparalleled. We were inspired and changed, students and staff alike. Mark is amazingly real. This message must be heard!"

> ERIC MORRIS
> Principal, Timothy Christian School
> Piscataway, New Jersey

"Mark Cahill is a gift to the whole body of Christ! Mark is a modern-day soul-winner who walks his talk and teaches others to do the same. I am never as challenged to win souls as I am when I am around him, listening to him or reading his material. This material and bold approach are anointed and will help get Christendom back to its primary purpose 'to seek and to save that which was lost.' Read and apply every word."

> MARK N. SHANER
> Youth Pastor, Central Community Church
> Wichita, Kansas

"In Ephesians 5:16, we're told to 'make the most of every opportunity.' I've been on staff with FCA for 15 years and had no idea how many witnessing opportunities I was passing by until I met Mark Cahill. Lots of folks have great intentions, but Cahill is truly an example of an individual who makes the most of every opportunity. He is the 'poster boy' for one-on-one evangelism! His countless stories and real-life illustrations will shame you and challenge you to begin seizing the everyday opportunities to comfortably speak out for our Lord Jesus Christ."

> STEVE WIGGINTON
> Kentuckiana Area Director,
> Fellowship of Christian Athletes

"Mark Cahill's burden for lost souls, his fervor and passion for all ages to know Christ personally, is unsurpassed. His presentation of evangelism is powerful, motivating, and most importantly, Christlike."

>Dan McMillan
>Principal, Loganville Christian Academy
>Loganville, Georgia

"If I wanted a bunch of teenagers or adults to get excited about sharing their faith in Jesus, I would seek out Mark Cahill to do the job. I have never encountered a man more totally sold out to his Lord than Mark. He, unlike many speakers and authors, walks the talk. He has spent hours with my high-school group walking the streets and sharing his faith. They have caught his fire and passion for the lost simply by being around him and listening to his teaching.

"No waitress, store owner, or airline passenger sneaks under the radar of Mark Cahill. The man is a bold witness 24/7. He is on a personal, passionate mission to make sure everyone hears the Gospel. He can motivate the most recent believer, shy personality, or biblical illiterate to share his faith and do it with joy and power. We need more Mark Cahills to stir us to action, to encourage us to proclaim Jesus anywhere, anytime, and to anyone."

>Richard King
>Youth Pastor, Mountain Park First Baptist Church
>Stone Mountain, Georgia

"Mark has a burning compassion for souls like I have seldom witnessed! He has a unique way of challenging people as well as equipping them to share their faith."

>Joe Wright
>Pastor, Central Christian Church
>Wichita, Kansas

One Thing You Can't Do In Heaven

Mark Cahill

"The truth shall make you free"

One Thing You Can't Do in Heaven

Copyright © 2002, 2003, 2004, 2005 by Mark Cahill.
All rights reserved.
No part of this publication may be reproduced, stored in a retrieval system, or transmitted by any means—electronic, mechanical, photographic (photocopying), recording, or otherwise—without prior permission in writing from the author *unless it is for the furtherance of the gospel of salvation and given away free*. Order additional copies at www.markcahill.org.

ISBN 978-0-9643665-8-9
Published by:
Biblical Discipleship Publishers
2212 Chisholm Trail
Rockwall, Texas 75002
www.biblicaldiscipleship.org

All Scripture quotations are from the Authorized (King James) Version of the Bible.

Interior illustrations are by Gustave Doré, *The Doré Bible Illustrations*, Dover Publications, Inc.

Previously published:
Genesis Publishing Group: ISBN 0-9749300-0-8.
Edited by Lynn Copeland
Cover and page design by Genesis Publishing Group
www.genesis-group.net

Ninth printing, June 2007
Fifth edition edited by N'omi Smith Orr

Printed in the United States of America

Presented to:

From:

On:

Very special thanks to:
Jesus Christ
for giving me a reason to live,
and a reason to die.

Thanks to:
Dad, Mom, Mike, Matt, Jill, Steve, Morgan, Holly, Christian, and all of my extended family. Brother Woody, Joanna, Ray, Sonya, Meg, Ed, Don, Jobe, JennaDee, and all the rest of the folks who have had a Christian influence in my life. Thanks to Joe White, Mike McCoy, Richard King, Jeff Myers, and David Noebel for giving me my start in the Christian speaking world. If I have forgotten your name here, please know that I have not forgotten you.

Contents

Introduction 11

1. South Beach 15
2. GET To! 22
3. Winning, Winning, Winning 31
4. Excuses, Excuses 48
5. Did You Get One of These? 62
6. If They're Breathing, They Need Jesus 73
7. Say What? 93
8. Guilty! 111
9. Four Deadly Questions 140
10. Good Answer! 149
11. A Pocket Full of Tickets 169
12. Is There Not a Cause? 182
13. Hit List 201
14. Dear Satan or Dear God 221

Therefore, when he was gone out, Jesus said, "Now is the Son of man glorified, and God is glorified in him."
John 13:31

INTRODUCTION

Three-hundred-million years from now, what will be the only thing that will matter? Will it matter how much money you made? Will it matter what kind of car you drove? Will it matter who won the NCAA football and basketball titles this year? Will it matter who you took to the homecoming dance?

Three-hundred-million years from now, the only thing that will matter is who is in heaven and who is in hell. And if that is the only thing that will matter then, that should be one of our greatest concerns now. Jesus tells us in Matthew 18:11, "The Son of Man has come to save that which was lost." If it is of the utmost importance for Jesus to reach the lost, shouldn't it be a major priority for you? The real question then is: What are you doing of significance today that will matter three-hundred-million-plus years from now?

Second Corinthians 5:10 assures us that "we must all appear before the judgment seat of Christ; that every one may receive the things done in his body, according to that he hath done, whether it be good or bad." Do you really believe, as a follower of the Lord Jesus Christ, that there will be a day on which you will stand before His throne? We will each go one-on-one with the God of this universe. Can you imagine that? Do you think it will matter on that day whether you boldly shared your faith with unbelievers, whether you told a very lost and dying world about Jesus—the only answer for a soul? Yes, it will. It will matter whether you shared the most precious thing you have with everyone you could.

I have envisioned standing before the throne of God, and I believe certain thoughts are going to hit me. When I look at Jesus, I think it will occur to me that He is more real than I ever imagined. I will be struck by how sinful and impure I am in front of Total Holiness. It will amaze me how beautiful Heaven is, well beyond what I could have ever dreamed. But then I think it will really hit me that I'll wish I would have shared Him a whole lot more than I ever did on earth.

If we could spend time with Peter and Paul, I wonder what advice they would give us. If we were able to talk with Spurgeon, Whitefield, Wesley, and Moody, what guidance would they offer? I truly believe they would tell us to give ourselves totally to reaching the lost no matter what the cost; to not look back but to boldly speak out for our Lord. Romans 10:13–15 says:

> For whosoever shall call upon the name of the Lord shall be saved. How then shall they call on him in whom they have not believed? and how shall they believe in him of whom they have not heard? and how shall they hear without a preacher? And how shall they preach, except they be sent? as it is written, How beautiful are the feet of them that preach the Gospel of peace, and bring glad tidings of good things!

That is what this book is about: sending every believer out with the confidence, boldness, and love of Jesus Christ to reach a very lost and dying world. People will not believe in Jesus and call upon Him for their salvation unless they hear about what He has done for them. And how can they hear unless each Christian takes the great name of Jesus to every person possible?

Over the last seven years, I have had the opportunity to witness to several thousand people individually. I have been humbled through that experience and by the lessons

Introduction

God has taught me along the way. This book distills what I've learned in those seven years, which I hope will shorten the learning curve for others. My prayer is that you will find this book to be very challenging, and yet encouraging. First Thessalonians 5:11 says, "Wherefore comfort yourselves together, and edify one another, even as also ye do." We all need encouragement to be the best that we can be for Jesus Christ. My intent is not to make you feel guilty because you have not been sharing your faith like you should. Instead, I hope through these pages to encourage you to be bold for the Lord. This book will challenge you that you have the only answer for eternity. And it will equip you to share that answer using very practical, biblical techniques for reaching the lost.

To help you use this book for personal or group study, we've prepared a Study Guide which you can download for free from www.markcahill.org. Going through the material as a group and discussing its ideas will help you to further build these principles into your life—so you can live them out.

Today, approximately 150,000 people will die. I wonder where each of them will spend eternity? Enjoy this book, and then step out of your comfort zone, trusting the Lord in what He can do through you. Always remember that, every time you step out of *your* comfort zone, you step right into *God's* comfort zone. Thanks for wanting to do something that will make a difference three-hundred-million-plus years from now!

And there appeared an angel unto him from Heaven, strengthening him.
Luke 22:43

Chapter 1

South Beach

"Every Christian is either a missionary or an impostor."
Charles Haddon Spurgeon

South Beach, Miami, Florida. If you have never been there, it is truly an amazing place. Beach, sun, sand, tans, Lamborghinis, drinking, drugs, nightlife, and sin—that's what South Beach is all about. It is wild, it is crazy, and it is America's version of Sodom and Gomorrah. And I just love going there! I know that sounds strange, but I try to get to South Beach at least once a year. The spiritual darkness there is unbelievable. So many people are hurting, and they are looking for truth and love. As a matter of fact, it is so dark there that it is easy for a believer's light to shine very brightly.

A couple of years ago I was in South Beach witnessing. I like to hit the streets around 8:00 p.m. and stay until about 4:00 a.m. It makes for an interesting, but very long, evening. One night as I was walking along a street, I saw a young woman sitting on top of a newspaper stand. I approached her and struck up a conversation, then I asked her this question: "When you die, what do you think is on the other side?"

She gave me a most interesting answer: "A whole bunch of naked women."

I have heard that answer from guys before, but never from a girl! As we talked, I learned that she was a seventeen-year-old Jewish girl who was struggling with lesbianism.

She opened up, and had a lot of very in-depth questions about God and sin. She had really thought about the eternal side of life. About halfway through the conversation, she admitted that her curfew was midnight; it was now 12:40 in the morning.

She explained that, as she was driving home to arrive before her curfew, something in her mind told her not to go home, but to go to South Beach instead. So she did. She then pointed a finger at me and said, "You are the whole reason that I came to South Beach tonight!"

My jaw almost hit the concrete. We typically think that people don't want to talk with us about eternity and Jesus, but that's just another lie from the devil. This young lady was searching for eternal truth, and God had her out long past her curfew to hear the information that she had truly been seeking. Psalm 145:18 says, "The Lord is nigh unto all them that call upon him, to all that call upon him in truth." God has placed an awareness of God's truth in the heart of every man and woman. No matter how deep people may push it down, it is still there. They know there is something more than this life's relativism. It is our job to help them find the truth of what is waiting for them in eternity, of who God is, and how they can commit to Him and live by His principles.

We typically think that people don't want to talk with us about eternity and Jesus, but that's just another lie from the devil.

As we continued to talk, one of her friends came out of an ice-cream parlor and sat down. She asked him, "Do you believe in this Jesus? What do you think about all this Jesus stuff?" This young lady was witnessing, and she wasn't even a believer yet!

Toward the end of our conversation, she looked at me and asked, "Are you an angel from God?"

I said that I couldn't be: I have an address, a phone number, etc. The Bible tells us to entertain strangers because we might be entertaining an angel without realizing it. Although I was a stranger to her, I was not a stranger to the world. What she was saying, though, was that God had touched her life, and He happened to use me to do that. What a humbling thought that the God of this universe would use fallen mankind to plant seeds in the hearts of the lost! Five times in my life someone has asked me if I was an angel from God. It is a little unnerving, but when we step out in faith and boldly share the good news of Jesus Christ with all the love we can, people will see Jesus through our lives.

One Thing You Can't Do in Heaven

I will never forget that young lady. But what would cause me to even want to talk with her that night? Here is one of those reasons—and it is a weighty piece of eternal truth. I can guarantee that there is one thing you cannot do in Heaven that you can do on earth. You can worship God in Heaven. You can praise God in Heaven. You can sing songs to God in Heaven. You can learn God's Word in Heaven. But one thing you cannot do in Heaven is share your faith with a non-believer. Why? Because everyone in Heaven is a believer. Do you realize that when you take your last breath, you will never again be able to talk with a lost person? Since that is true, shouldn't it be a priority of your life to reach out to all the lost people on earth while you can?

Auburn University gave me a four-year basketball scholarship for one very simple reason. I don't say this to be cocky, but I can shoot a basketball pretty well. I can take that orange ball and put it in the goal. Some people say I was born with the talent. I don't believe that, although I definitely have athletic talent wired into me. The real reason I can shoot a basketball pretty well is hours upon hours upon hours of practice. All I did as a kid was shoot basketball, and if you do something often enough you get pretty good at it. So, if we can't witness in Heaven and can witness only on earth, what is the only way we will ever become good at it? Practice. Practice. Practice.

I firmly believe that witnessing is a learned talent. God burdens our hearts to reach the lost, but we must get out there and start practicing those conversations. The funny thing is, though, the more you practice, the easier it becomes.

In That Very Hour

For the past four years, I have gotten into a conversation with every person I have sat next to on an airplane flight. I do this because I know I have to practice sharing my faith in order to improve. And since I pray for those people before we meet, I don't consider them strangers, but friends I haven't met yet. If God seats a believer next to me, I encourage that person to be a bold man or woman of God. If He puts a nonbeliever next to me, then I give the person the best news ever heard!

After taking my seat on a flight out of Colorado Springs, I introduced myself to the man next to me and we began to chat. He had in his hands a very thick book with very small print. I asked him what he was reading—and why he would want to read such a hefty book. It was a title by Dostoevski that he had read in college twenty years earlier, he told me, and he felt that he needed to read it again. I was thinking, *This guy has too much free time on his hands!*

He worked at the Pentagon for the Ballistic Missile Defense Operations. He was a very interesting man and was

SOUTH BEACH

quite conservative in his outlook. We hit it right off, and shared the same viewpoint on numerous issues. The problem was, he would not close his book. He didn't look at it, but he kept it open on his lap. When someone closes his book, it signals his interest in getting into a good conversation with you. We talked for an hour; the book was still open.

So I said, "Can I ask you an interesting question?"

He replied, "Sure."

"When you die, what do you think is on the other side? What do you think is out there when we walk out of here?"

He was not sure. The book was still open, but we kept talking. Suddenly he took his plane ticket, used it as a bookmark, and closed the book! Then the conversation really took off. The rest of the flight we talked about eternal matters. At one point he said, "I get the feeling that you are just walking me along!" We both laughed. I said that it might seem like that, but I do believe that all of this is very logical and straightforward. At the end of the flight, he said, "I want to thank you for something. You're not one of those zealots or fanatics, and I really like that."

God burdens our hearts to reach the lost, but we must get out there and start practicing those conversations.

I laughed, "Well, if you got to know me, you might have a different opinion!" Then I added, "But what I think you are trying to say is that I didn't take my religion and shove it down your throat."

He said, "That's exactly what I'm trying to say." I got his business card, and later wrote him a letter and sent him a book. We had this conversation six weeks before the World Trade Center and Pentagon attack; I have since wondered what happened to him.

Little did I know that the living God was going to place a man so hungry for spiritual truth next to me on that flight. All I had to do was get into the conversation and watch it go from there. Jesus says, in Luke 12:12, "For the Holy Ghost shall teach you in the same hour what ye ought to say." The Holy Spirit is very faithful to take us all the way through a conversation and to give us plenty of things to say. All we must do is get in "that same hour." Let the Lord take you into those opportunities, and He will show you how faithful He really is.

There are only two times to share the Gospel with people: in season and out of season. Any other time would be wrong!

Second Timothy 4:2–8 is a powerful part of the Bible. In verse 2, Paul tells us, "Preach the word; be instant in season, out of season; reprove, rebuke, exhort with all longsuffering and doctrine." Remember that there are only two times to share the Gospel with people: in season and out of season. Any other time would be wrong! That means we should be prepared to preach the Word at all times, and go for it. Also realize that when we stand in front of God, none of us will say that we shared His Son too much. But many of us will realize that we shared His Son much too little during our time on earth.

Practice. Practice. Practice. Can you think of someone you need to practice with today? I am not referring to role-playing, but to an actual conversation with a friend. Go for it. You will be glad you did.

Now that we know one thing we can't do in Heaven, what can give us the boldness that we all should have in the Lord? The next chapter will show how we can train our minds to start viewing opportunities from the Lord in a different way.

And he that betrayed him had given them a token, saying, "Whomsoever I shall kiss, that same is he…"
Mark 14:44

CHAPTER 2

GET TO!

"To be laughed at is no great hardship to me. I can delight in scoffs and jeers. Caricatures, lampoons, and slanders are my glory. But that you should turn from your own mercy, this is my sorrow. Spit on me, but, oh, repent! Laugh at me, but, oh, believe in my Master! Make my body as the dirt of the streets, but damn not your own souls!"
CHARLES HADDON SPURGEON

I firmly believe that we must change our mindset about sharing our faith. We must view it as the awesome opportunity that it is and not as some sort of drudgery. It should be a joyful activity that we can't wait to do instead of the worst part of our week. So how can that be done?

God impressed my heart a few years ago in a very simple but life-changing way. Often when we wake up late on Sunday morning and are tired, we think that we have "got" to go to church. That is completely the wrong perspective. It is not that we have "got" to go to church, but that we "GET" to go to church!

It is a privilege to gather with fellow believers and worship our great God and Savior. By just changing a vowel, it goes from being a task to being an opportunity! There are believers in China who literally walk six hours to go to church, and they don't have "McChurch" for thirty minutes! They thoroughly worship the Lord, and then they walk six hours back home. We consider it "suffering" when we have

GET TO!

to drive to church in the rain! We must develop the mindset that we "GET" to go to church.

We may realize, at eleven o'clock at night, that we haven't had a quiet time of prayer that day. It is not that we have "got" to pray, but we "GET" to pray to the Almighty God of this universe! Isn't it amazing that the God who is in total control of this universe will take time out of His day to hear us pray to Him? He can't wait to communicate with us and listen to our heart. It is not a chore to pray, but an incredible opportunity. We should so desire to communicate with our heavenly Father that we "pray without ceasing" (1 Thessalonians 5:17).

Sometimes we realize very late at night that we haven't read our Bible yet that day. We have the mindset that we have "got" to read the Bible, but we must not view it as a chore. It's not that we have "got" to read our Bible, but we "GET" to read the holy Word of God. We have the chance to nourish our spirit with eternal food at any point during the day that we choose. Jesus said, "Man shall not live by bread alone, but by every word that proceedeth out of the mouth of God" (Matthew 4:4).

Isn't it amazing that the God who is in total control of this universe will take time out of His day to hear us pray to Him?

One time I was speaking in California and staying at Lake Arrowhead Resort. Each night I would return late from my speaking engagements. The second night there, I got into a conversation with the night security guard. Luis was a very interesting young man. He was twenty years old, and was struggling after a breakup with his girlfriend. He really thought she was the person he was going to marry. As we chatted, he told me that he had made a commitment to Christ when he was younger, but that he wasn't into it as much as he should be. He couldn't go to church on Sunday because of his work schedule. I asked him if he had a Bible, which he did. I then asked if he had time to read at work. He replied that just about all he did at work was read. Lying on his desk were *Rolling Stone*, *People*, and *Spin* magazines. So I told him that if he brought his Bible in to work and read just three-and-a-half chapters a day, he would be able to read the whole Bible in one year. Setting aside fifteen to thirty minutes a day is all it takes to read God's Word once through each year. He said he would do that.

The next two nights when I came in, Luis wasn't there. My last night in town, Luis was on duty and we had another good chat. I asked him if he had brought his Bible in and read it. He told me that he did and had been reading it each night. He had read twenty chapters the first night alone! He said that, since he closed the Bible two nights earlier, he had not had one jealous thought about his girlfriend.

Whatever situation you are facing, God's Word has the answer. Second Timothy 3:16-17 assures us, "All scripture is given by inspiration of God, and is profitable for doctrine, for reproof, for correction, for instruction in righteousness: That the man of God may be perfect, thoroughly furnished unto all good works." What a privilege it is to "GET" to read God's Word.

Many times we have the mindset that we have "got" to tithe our money to God. We most definitely have the wrong mindset. It is not that we have "got" to tithe and give our money to the work of the Lord, but that we "GET" to! As the economy has slowed recently, many pastors around the country are reporting that tithes are down significantly. All I know is that when times get tough we ought to give more, not less. If I need to make a cut in my budget, it cannot be in the money that I give to the work of God. I have cheated God in the past with my tithes and offerings, but no more.

A friend of mine supports twenty-five missionaries each month. When his finances got tight, he took out a loan to pay the missionaries that month! I was so humbled by what he did.

He knows the importance of giving with all that you have to the work of the Lord. Luke 6:38 tells us, "Give, and it shall be given unto you; good measure, pressed down, and shaken together, and running over, shall men give into your bosom. For with the same measure that ye mete withal it shall be measured to you again." In Malachi 3:8–11, God says:

> Will a man rob God? Yet ye have robbed me. But ye say, Wherein have we robbed thee? In tithes and offerings. Ye are cursed with a curse: for ye have robbed me, even this whole nation. Bring ye all the tithes into the storehouse, that there may be meat in mine house, and prove me now herewith, saith the Lord of hosts, if I will not open you the windows of Heaven, and pour you out a blessing, that there shall not be room enough to receive it. And I will rebuke the devourer for your sakes, and he shall not destroy the fruits of your ground; neither shall your vine cast her fruit before the time in the field, saith the Lord of hosts.

Giving back to God is a privilege. We must learn to view it that way. As I speak at different events, I find it interesting to observe the various styles of worshiping God. Apparently, many people consider it a chore to sing loud and from the heart to the Lord that we love. They appear to have the mindset that they have "got" to praise and worship God. Instead, they should realize that we "GET" to worship the King of kings with our entire being!

Psalm 150 gives us a good example of how we should worship Him:

Praise ye the Lord.

Praise God in his sanctuary: praise him in the firmament of his power.

Praise him for his mighty acts: praise him according to his excellent greatness.

Praise him with the sound of the trumpet: praise him with the psaltery and harp.

Praise him with the timbrel and dance: praise him with stringed instruments and organs.

Praise him upon the loud cymbals: praise him upon the high sounding cymbals.

Let every thing that hath breath praise the Lord.

Praise ye the Lord.

By the way, when we die, it is not that we have "got" to go to Heaven, but we "GET" to go to Heaven! I am praying that the Holy Spirit will use this book to change your mindset from one in which you have "got" to share your faith, to realizing that you "GET" to share your faith with all the lost people you can find until you get to Heaven.

When you die, it isn't that you've "got" to go to Heaven by yourself. When you die and "GET" to go to Heaven, you "GET" to bring as many people as you want to! We must have that mindset.

There is something else we must realize as we share our faith: the value of other people in the eyes of Almighty God. What is a soul worth? God said that He made mankind in His own image and likeness (Genesis 1:26). Every soul is of infinite value to God. Once we understand that, it will keep us on the edge of our seat and on the tips of our toes to share the good news of Jesus with every lost soul on this planet.

In Mark 16:15, Jesus tells us to "Go ye into all the world, and preach the Gospel to every creature." One great place to go out witnessing is at events such as state fairs. While at a state fair in Georgia, I had a great conversation with three wild-looking teenagers. They were tattooed, pierced, and wearing crazy-looking clothes. Near the end of the talk, I told them that they were fearfully and wonderfully made by God—that they had been knit together piece by piece in their mother's womb. I asked, "How special does that make you?"

They responded, "Pretty special."

I then asked, "Do you know that you were made in the image of the God of this universe? Do you know how special that makes you?"

They replied, "Very special."

I agreed, "You are very special! If anyone ever tells you any different, they are 100-percent wrong—and don't you ever forget that!"

You should have seen their eyes light up! I didn't just view the outward appearance, I saw the value of the inward person. Because I knew how special they were in the eyes of God, I wanted them to hear the truth about His Son, Jesus Christ.

Because I saw how special they were in the eyes of God, I couldn't wait for them to know the truth about His Son, Jesus Christ.

How do you see your coworkers? How do you see the people who walk past you every day? We must view them as valuable, as the Lord does; then there won't be anything we wouldn't do to help them come to a saving knowledge of the

Lord Jesus Christ. Going into the whole world to preach the Gospel will be a joy.

It may seem very intimidating to think about going out witnessing to strangers, but that's a great way to meet the lost—and it works!

I was asked to do a retreat for the youth group of a large church. The youth pastor and I were planning to hold it at a local hotel and then take the teens out witnessing at a mall. But once the pastor caught wind of our plans, he was none too happy. He told the youth pastor that that type of witnessing doesn't work. Christians must build relationships first and not do "cold-call" witnessing. The youth pastor then decided to take the teens to a retreat center far away from civilization (and any actual lost people) so they could learn how to share their faith. On Sunday afternoon after the retreat, one of the teens decided to go the mall to witness, and got into a conversation with an Iranian man.

The man said, "It's very interesting that you're talking with me. One of the reasons I came to America was to find out more about Christianity. Matter of fact, I just bought a Bible yesterday."

During the conversation, the teenager asked, "Have you ever been to a Christian church before?"

He said "no," so the teen asked, "Would you like to come with me next week to my church?"

The man said, "That would be great."

Isn't it nice to know that that type of witnessing doesn't work!

In the next chapter, I'll share with you something that the Lord impressed upon me—a truth that changed me from being a wimp for Jesus to being a much bolder witness for the Lord. It is also the truth that touches many people's lives when I speak around the country. It encourages believers to

GET TO!

step out of their comfort zone when it comes to witnessing, and step right into God's comfort zone. They are never the same again! Let's see what changes so many lives.

CHAPTER 3

WINNING, WINNING, WINNING

"If there be any one point in which the Christian church ought to keep its fervor at a white heat, it is concerning missions. If there be anything about which we cannot tolerate lukewarmness, it is the matter of sending the gospel to a dying world."
CHARLES HADDON SPURGEON

Being a counselor at a Christian summer camp is always a fun thing to do. It is a way to grow in your faith and make an eternal investment in the lives of others. One of the great camps in America is Kanakuk Kamps in Branson, Missouri (www.kanakuk.com). I worked there as a counselor a few years ago.

The group I was in had ten campers and three counselors. Each night we would have devotionals in our cabin. One afternoon, as I was praying about a topic for that night's devotional, the Lord laid on my heart to talk about witnessing and evangelism. I thought that was a little strange since I wasn't one to share my faith a lot; but when God begins to lead, I have learned that it is a good idea to follow! So that night as we talked about witnessing, I asked the guys, "What are the only three possible things that can happen when we share our faith?" The correct answer they gave was: 1) the person can accept Jesus Christ; 2) the person can reject Jesus Christ; or 3) we can plant a seed. After we talked about each of the possibilities, we came up with a chart that looked like the following.

ACCEPT	PLANT SEED	REJECT
GOOD	GOOD	BAD
WINNING	WINNING	LOSING

We determined that accepting Jesus was a good situation, planting a seed was a good situation, and rejecting Jesus was a bad situation. Another way to look at it was that accepting Christ was a winning situation, planting a seed was a winning situation, and being rejected was a losing situation. We concluded that 66 percent of the time that we share our faith it is a winning situation. Aren't those pretty good odds? Two-thirds of the time that we share our faith, we literally can't lose!

If you know anything about sports, wouldn't Shaquille O'Neal take that from the free-throw line when he shoots a basketball? Of course he would! He is a terrible free-throw shooter; he shoots in the 40 percent range. He would take 66 percent in a second when it comes to shooting free-throws, but many of us won't take it when it comes to witnessing because we are so afraid that we'll be rejected when we stand up for Jesus Christ. The biggest fear most people say they have about witnessing is the fear of being rejected.

Little did I know that the very next day the God of the universe was going to change my life forever. I was sitting on a dock in the middle of a lake when God spoke to my heart like never before. I was reading 1 Peter 4:14. which says, "If ye be reproached for the name of Christ, happy are ye; for the spirit of glory and of God resteth upon you: On their part he is evil spoken of, but on your part he is glorified." Just think about that for a moment. If we ever get rejected in the name of Jesus, we will be blessed and the glory of God will rest upon us. If you could have the glory of God shine in your life and be reflected onto others, would you want that? We all would want that as much as possible! One way that will happen is if we are rejected in the name of Jesus.

God wasn't done with me yet. Luke 6:22-23 says, "Blessed are ye, when men shall hate you, and when they shall separate you from their company, and shall reproach you, and cast out your name as evil, for the Son of man's sake. Rejoice ye in that day, and leap for joy: for, behold, your reward is great in Heaven: for in the like manner did their fathers unto the prophets."

Do you realize that when you get rejected in the name of Jesus, God has rewards waiting for you in Heaven that will make any earthly reward seem like chump change? That is truly amazing.

After I spoke at a Christian high school in Mobile, Alabama, a group of students decided to go witnessing at the malls and at the beach. They were rarely shot down by someone, but if they were, they would make the sound *cha-ching* (like a cash register). They would ring up their rewards in Heaven, and then give each other a "high five" and move on to the next person. They decided to take the Word of God literally and not let anything get them down, but just be bold for the Lord.

When I was speaking at a Fellowship of Christian Athletes leadership conference in Lexington, Kentucky, the teens and college students went witnessing door-to-door one afternoon. One group went to the first house on the street and were rejected. They rang up their rewards in Heaven, gave each other a "high five," and moved on. At the next house no one was home. At the next house they were rejected. Next house no one was home. After eight houses, they became discouraged. They considered quitting and trying again another day, but they remembered their reward in Heaven and kept pressing on. At the ninth house was a man sitting on his porch in a rocking chair, drinking a beer. As they began talking with him, he quickly told them they were wasting their time. When they asked why, he replied, "Because there is no way God can forgive me of all my sins."

We know that is not a true statement. But Satan will lie to people to make them think their sins are so bad that they cannot be forgiven. The students asked the man what he had done that was so bad that God would not forgive him.

While he was in Vietnam, he explained, he was dropped into towns and villages where he would indiscriminately kill women and children. Sometimes he would put his gun behind him and shoot people behind his back like it was a game.

The students began to minister to him and show him the love of God. They talked about sin and the cleansing blood of Jesus. Forty-five minutes later the man said, "I really need this Jesus you are talking about."

They prayed with him as he accepted Jesus. The teens reported later that when he lifted his head, he had a glow on his face that they had never seen before. He said, "I just feel like reading my Bible! I just feel like going to church! That's all I feel like doing."

What an amazing story! But this would not have happened if those kids had given up and not pressed on in the Lord, if they had been more concerned about rejection than about their reward in Heaven.

But after God showed me those two verses, I had begun that night's devotions by saying that I had misled them the previous night. I'd said we had a 66-percent chance of a winning situation when we share our faith. Then I shared those two verses with them, and their eyes opened wide as they too realized the mistake we had made. Now that we know those two verses, let's see how the chart changes.

Accept	Plant Seed	Reject
Good	Good	Good
Winning	Winning	Winning

Just by knowing the Word of God, we learned that every time we share our faith it is a winning situation. I don't ever have to worry again about Satan trying to talk me out of witnessing, because the Word of God says that I can't lose doing it. It is a winning situation every single time!

Let Satan Draw Them Together
While witnessing at a mall in Denver, I started a conversation with two teenagers. One of them didn't want anything to do with me so he stood to the side while I talked with his friend. The other teen told me that they had just left a satanic cult. They had seen animal sacrifices at some of their meetings, so I decided to ask him a crazy question: "Have you ever seen a human sacrifice at one of your meetings?" Be careful what you ask because you may just get an answer.

He said, "Yes, I have." He then described what they did with a newborn baby. I was shocked at what he was saying, but I could tell from his eyes that he was serious.

I began to witness to him about sin and his need for Jesus Christ. There was no way I could lose in sharing my faith, since it is a winning situation every single time. We not only had a great conversation, but I had a chance to talk with him again before he left the mall.

Aren't you a little bit angry at what Satan is doing to the fifteen- and sixteen-year-olds of the world? Are you mad enough yet to want to do something about it? If you ever want to find a good place to witness, just see where Satan is working hard and go there. He is working very hard on middle-schoolers and high-schoolers. So why don't we make sure that we are reaching them with the truth, before Satan reaches them with a lie?

One gentleman I know has a motto when it comes to witnessing: "Let Satan draw them together, and we will witness to them." What a motto! Let Satan do all the work of bringing people together, then we can just show up and share the Gospel. Malls, sporting events, coffee shops, college campuses, tailgate parties before football games, concerts, art festivals, music festivals, festivals of any kind, parks, spring break gatherings, beaches, bar sections of towns, laundromats, bus stations, etc.—all of these are great places where we can witness and hand out tracts.

Atlanta, Georgia, hosts a big annual festival the first weekend of May called Music Midtown. It usually has about a dozen stages and hosts some of the top secular bands for three days. I put it on my schedule each year and go there to witness. This year approximately 300,000 people attended the event. God gave me the chance to witness to more than fifty people during the weekend, and to hand out 3,000 tracts about Jesus. What a weekend! It is one of my favorite weekends of the year. Last year at the festival a man pointed his finger at me and said, "I know you." He told me that I had witnessed to him two years ago at that festival, and he saw me again last year. This year he stopped to talk. How he remembered me from a couple of years ago I will never know, but we serve a great God who is working on hearts in ways we can't even imagine.

Winning, Winning, Winning

Piedmont Park in downtown Atlanta hosts four really good festivals each year. They are excellent places to witness, because people who just hang out and are killing time are eager to chat. One festival is the second-largest gay-and-lesbian festival in the United States. For the last several years I have gone there and witnessed. You might initially think that it wouldn't be such a great place for that, but it is actually a very easy place to witness. There is a lot of death in the gay community. Homosexuals often think about eternity because so many of their friends die.

One man I talked with at the festival in 1999 told me that twenty years earlier he and eighty friends had a group photo taken at a gay bar in Atlanta. He said that a week ago he had looked at the photo again. He held up five fingers as he explained that out of eighty guys, only five were still living! At the end of our conversation he said, "Thank you for being down here and sharing what you believe, and thank you *so much* for how you're doing it."

Let's not separate ourselves from the lost, but take our light into the darkness and watch the Lord work in amazing ways.

Homosexuals tend to be the only group of people that Christians look down on and treat like the scum of the earth. We don't do that with liars, thieves, blasphemers, prisoners, etc., but we often do with homosexuals. Once we witness to homosexuals eye to eye and realize how much they truly need Jesus, we can show them the appropriate love, and they will be receptive to our message.

This past year on the same weekend as the gay festival, on the other side of town, was the annual three-day festival of contemporary Christian music. That illustrates how too many people lead the Christian life: they completely separate themselves from the lost and don't engage them with the truth. If just a small group of people from the Christian festival had gone to the gay festival, it would have taken only a few hours to talk with everyone about Jesus, and then they could have returned to their Christian concerts rejoicing that they shared the Good News. Let's not separate ourselves from the lost, but take our light into the darkness and watch the Lord work in amazing ways.

Ruffling Feathers

While coming home from a festival at Piedmont Park, I felt that I had not done enough witnessing. I was passing through a part of town where prostitutes hang out, and for some reason I decided to stop. I pulled up to a woman, chatted with her briefly, then offered her ten dollars to talk for ten minutes. Prostitutes work for money and won't talk very long if there is no pay involved.

"Are you a cop?" she asked suspiciously.

I replied, "No."

"Are you recording this?"

"No!"

She agreed to get into the car, and we drove around and talked for a few minutes. It didn't go well, so I dropped her off. I still felt that I had not done enough witnessing, so I picked up another prostitute—and we ended up talking for thirty minutes! This woman had a six-year-old child. Do you think prostitutes enjoy their lives? They don't; they hate their lifestyles.

One woman told me that she made $500 a day prostituting herself, and spent $300 a day on crack cocaine! God did not design any of us to live a life like that. Some prostitutes are so miserable that they're crying their eyes out when we finish talking.

WINNING, WINNING, WINNING

Whenever I tell this story, it ruffles people's feathers. One person asked, "What if someone from your church drove by and saw you picking up a prostitute?"

I answered, "If people from my church saw me doing that, they would probably say, 'There goes Mark again witnessing to a prostitute; let's pray for him.' Then they would probably pray that if I had picked up that prostitute for the wrong reason, the Spirit would convict me so that I would not do anything to discredit the ministry of the Lord Jesus Christ."

Why are we so concerned about what other people think of us? It was okay for Jesus to be a friend of the tax collectors, prostitutes, and sinners, but it is apparently not okay for us. I have received letters from people who were shocked that I would encourage others to witness to prostitutes.

I asked one person if she witnesses to prostitutes. She doesn't. Does anyone in her family witness to prostitutes? No. Does anyone at her church witness to prostitutes? No. I then explained, if she doesn't witness to prostitutes, if no one in her family does, and if no one in her church does, then who will witness to these people? God loves them just as much as He does us "regular" people, and they need the good news of Jesus brought to them.

I confess that I didn't handle the situation the right way the night I witnessed to those prostitutes. I should have had someone else in the car with me. Even better would have been to get out of the car.

The best approach, I believe, would be for women, not men, to witness to prostitutes. But do you see where my heart is? I want every person I will ever meet to be in a relationship with Jesus.

After I finished speaking at the University of Central Florida at an event called "Undivided," about thirty people came up to me. They said they were going to go witnessing that night and needed some tract booklets. I asked where they were going. Ten of them were going to one bar section of Orlando, ten to another bar section, and ten to where the prostitutes hang out.

I asked one guy, "Are you sure you want to do that?"

"It's okay," he assured me. "My church witnesses to the prostitutes all the time."

I said, "My kind of church!"

When you discover that every time you share your faith it is a winning situation, you just can't wait to find lost people to talk with.

I taught the "winning, winning, winning" strategy one Sunday at a very nice, small church in St. Augustine, Florida. In the audience that morning was a professor from a local college. He was so enthralled with the teaching that when he and his wife went to Wal-Mart after church, he walked right up to a biker on a Harley-Davidson and began sharing his faith. His wife said that it was the longest trip they ever took to Wal-Mart!

The pastor of the church told me that he and his wife used to go witnessing on dates. If you decide to date rather than court, why does a date have to involve going to a movie or a party? Why can't a date consist of going to a mall to witness?

When the youth group and I went witnessing in downtown St. Augustine on Sunday and Monday nights, the pastor went with us. He said he had forgotten how much fun witnessing really was!

Winning, Winning, Winning

People Are Listening

In an airport one day, I was handing out tract booklets on the way to my flight. After I handed one guy a tract, he asked, "Do you remember me?"

I replied apologetically, "Well…I meet a lot of people."

He said, "I used to collect trash in your neighborhood in Stone Mountain."

When I would visit my parents there, I would sometimes see the trash collectors come by. I am very thankful that I don't do that for a living, so I try to encourage and bless those guys whenever I can. I often go out and talk with them, and sometimes give them tracts. They love talking basketball so we would often talk "hoops."

One time I grabbed some money and tracts, and gave each guy $7 and a tract booklet. I told them that I wanted to buy them lunch that day, but that the information in the booklet was much more important. I wonder how many people have ever done that for them? We need to do crazy things in love for the lost around us. They will never forget it!

At the airport the guy told me, "I saw you on ESPN Classic the other day." (You know you are getting old when you are not on ESPN anymore, but on ESPN Classic!) ESPN Classic did a one-hour special on Charles Barkley, a famous basketball player. Charles and I were on the same team together at Auburn University during our college years. Somehow they had dug up my name on the Internet and wanted me to give them some fresh stories about Charles. I remember two things about the interview: First, I tried to work Jesus into every answer so that no matter what was cut, there would still be some mention of Jesus in the interview. (Of course, I couldn't really do that, but I tried!) Second, the gentleman who interviewed me was Jewish. After the interview, I asked him a spiritual question, and we talked about it for fifteen minutes.

He then asked, "How do you know so much about what you believe?"

I thought that was an interesting question. Shouldn't we know a lot about what we believe? The more we know and the more we share in love, the more we find that people are listening. I later wrote him a letter and sent him a book (*God Doesn't Believe in Atheists,* by Ray Comfort), and we shall see one day what the Lord did with that seed.

At a mall one time, a man walked up to me and asked, "Do you remember me? You shared Jesus with me two years ago in this mall. Two months after that, I committed my life to Jesus and now I am living my life for Him!" He was so excited. Be bold about sharing what you believe. People are listening!

God opened a great door for me to speak to Clemson University's Fellowship of Christian Athletes. Each year the students go to Daytona Beach for a mission trip during spring break. Now, that sounds like a good spring break—not wasting a week of precious time, but using it for the Lord. The students work at places such as homeless shelters and juvenile detention centers. I spoke to them about witnessing, and at night we went out to talk with folks. The night we arrived was a Saturday—St. Patrick's day. What a great day for witnessing! Four college students and I hit the streets at about midnight to witness. At around 3:30 a.m. we walked up to two guys on motorcycles. The guy I began to talk with told me that a year earlier he had been going 120 mph on his bike when he lost control and hit a tree. He had also been shot two different times, one of which was self-inflicted. The previous week, his best friend had been riding his bike at 120 mph down a street in Daytona when a drunk driver pulled out in front of him. His friend died after ramming into the side of a Ford Explorer, which then flipped four times. You will be amazed at what you encounter when you step out in faith and begin conversations.

This biker was an atheist. Ten minutes into the conversation, he asked me to prove that there was a God. As I went through one of the basic proofs that I use (which I'll cover in Chapter 10), he nodded and agreed, "Now that's a good point." As we finished talking he told me, "I've learned an awful lot in this conversation." People are waiting to hear the truth if we will lovingly share it with them.

At 4:00 a.m., the students and I went back to our hotel. Half an hour later, I decided to get something out of my car. In the lobby of the hotel were four teens who were staring at me as I walked past them to my car. They were still there when I came back in, so I asked if I could do anything for them. One asked if I had a quarter for a phone call.

I checked my pockets and realized that I had emptied all my change onto the dresser in my room. So I said, "No, I don't have a quarter, but you guys can come up to my room and use my cell phone."

They were excited about that, so they jumped up and got on the elevator with me. As we were riding up to my room, one of the teens asked, "You know who we are going to call, don't you? We're going to call a stripper!"

"A stripper!"

"Yes, and you can join us if you want to."

I told the guys they had one problem—I'm a minister. You should have seen their eyes! I wish I'd had a video camera.

One guy said, "Oh...does that mean we can't use your cell phone?"

I didn't want to lose these guys, because it was obvious that we needed to have a conversation. So I handed each one a tract booklet, and said that if they read it they could use my phone.

They fulfilled their part of the bargain, so when we got to my room I let them make their call. As God would have it, they couldn't reach the stripper. So we began to talk about life. Just as I swung the conversation to the supernatural side, there was a knock on my door—it was two guys asking for the stripper. Unbelievable!

Somehow they all knew each other, so two of the teens went outside to talk with them. The other two stayed in the room, and we got into a serious conversation about Jesus. One teen said that he was able to have sex with a girl the night before just by giving her a cheap plastic necklace. I could see the emptiness in his eyes. As we began to get very serious, there was another knock on the door. It was the first two teens asking for their friends.

I told them, "They will be out in a minute."

I closed the door and went back to the conversation. There was another knock on the door.

I called, "They will be out in a minute."

Then there was a third knock on the door. The eighteen-year-old I was talking with went to the door, said that he would be out in a few minutes, and closed the door on his friends! God was working on this guy, and he really wanted to talk. I heard some noise at my door but didn't think much about it. I had the opportunity to pray with these two teens —not for salvation, because they didn't want to make a commitment, but just to let them hear someone pray for them. Do that as often as you can. It means so much to people.

I walked them to the door and said good-bye. As I looked back at the door, I realized what the other two guys had done. With a thick pencil they had written on my door "Smoke Reefer," "The Antichrist," "Satan Rules," "666," etc.

I yelled down the hall and told the two teens to come back. "Why don't you guys explain this to me?"

One guy blamed it on a friend who wasn't there. I told them that their friends should not have done that. When I grabbed some soap and a towel and began to clean my door, the guy on whom God seemed to be working said, "No, you shouldn't be doing that." He went inside my room to get a washcloth and soap and began washing my door for me! God was certainly touching that boy's heart. I told him it was okay, that I would finish it; then we parted company.

I told this story while I was speaking to the college students the next day, and one student suggested that God was keeping Satan out of the room, stuck right at the door, so that he could not interrupt the conversation inside the room. I do believe that is exactly what God was doing. The more you step out in faith and trust Him, the more amazing things you will see Him do.

Take a Stand

A couple of days later while speaking to the college students in Daytona Beach, my left knee began to swell—and swell!—and I couldn't put any pressure on my leg. So, being a typical guy, I asked for a chair so I could sit down to finish my talk. Afterwards, because I couldn't walk, someone suggested going to the emergency room.

Although I am not a big fan of doctors, I didn't see any other option at that point. So about ten college students piled into a van and took me to the emergency room. Along the way, I told the students that I was finally old enough and wise enough to realize that this whole situation didn't have anything to do with my knee. Instead, God was sending us to this emergency room for a reason, so we should find out what it was.

When the students walked into that dark hospital, they let their lights shine very brightly and ministered to people in an amazing way. One girl began to minister to a man who was suicidal. She did a wonderful job. Two others got to lead two people to Jesus in the middle of the emergency room!

The only time we lose is when we don't share our faith. Every other time it is a winning situation.

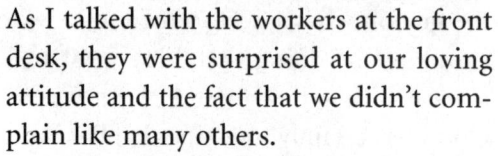

As I talked with the workers at the front desk, they were surprised at our loving attitude and the fact that we didn't complain like many others.

One woman said, "I was grouchy and grumpy, and then you walked into this place!" She wanted to have a terrible day, and we just wouldn't let her!

When we left, the seven workers at the front desk watched us as we walked out. These college students had discovered that every time they shared their faith they couldn't lose, so they took a bold, loving stand for Jesus.

We have now learned, straight from the Bible, that every time we share our faith it is a winning situation. The rest of this book won't make any sense unless you can answer this simple question: If every time we share our faith it is a winning situation, what is the only time we lose when it comes to witnessing? The only time we lose is when we don't share our faith. Every other time it is a winning situation. Now that we know that, let's look at some of the excuses we use that keep us from taking a very bold stand for our God who took a very bold stand on a cross just for you and me!

> And when they had platted a crown of thorns, they put it upon his head, and a reed in his right hand: and they bowed the knee before him, and mocked him, saying, "Hail, King of the Jews!"
> Matthew 27:29

Chapter 4

Excuses, Excuses

"I would sooner bring one sinner to Jesus Christ than unravel all the mysteries of the divine Word, for salvation is the one thing we are to live for."
Charles Haddon Spurgeon

Oswald J. Smith said, "Oh my friends, we are loaded down with countless church activities, while the real work of the church, that of evangelizing the world and winning the lost, is almost entirely neglected!" Don't neglect the call of the church to reach the lost. As one preacher put it, "God's top priority is the salvation of every single soul." We should desire to be used by God in what really matters to His heart.

Yet, although we know we *should* witness, there are many reasons why we don't boldly step out and share our faith. Let's look at some of those reasons, and see if any will hold weight when we stand in front of God one day.

Fear of Being Rejected

Are you more worried about what people think of you, or about what God thinks of you? Too many times believers worry what others think. However, when we are witnessing to people, what is the worst thing they can do to us? They can kill us and send us to Heaven. Is that such a bad thing? Philippians 1:21 says, " For to me to live is Christ, and to die is gain. " We live for Christ, and we die for Christ. That is the life of a true believer and disciple of Jesus Christ.

Excuses, Excuses

In Galatians 1:10 Paul says, "For do I now persuade men, or God? or do I seek to please men? for if I yet pleased men, I should not be the servant of Christ." As believers in Jesus Christ, we should live to please Him and no one else. Be focused on Christ in every area of your life, and God will do amazing things through you.

As we learned in Chapter 3, God shows us in the Holy Scriptures that every time we share our faith it is a winning situation. That truth took away my fear of rejection, as it has for countless others around the country. Let it do the same for you.

Don't Know How To

Another primary reason for not witnessing, according to surveys, is that people feel they don't know how to. But consider this: Didn't someone lead you to Jesus? If so, then you actually do know how to lead someone to the Lord. One eighth-grade student of mine led one of her best friends to Jesus. The very next day that girl led one of her public-school friends to Jesus—and she had been a believer for one day! She learned how to share her faith from the girl who led her to Christ.

The Bible gives us some great ways to share our faith. In John 4, Jesus talked with the woman at the well first about natural water, then about living water. He went from a natural topic to a spiritual one. In Acts 17, when Paul was giving his sermon on Mars Hill, he mentioned an altar he saw with an inscription, "To the unknown God." He took something natural around him and turned it into a supernatural conversation. So how can this work for us?

Think of an event around you that might involve death, and use it to spark a conversation about eternity. For example, I may ask people what they thought about the Columbine High School shooting. Everyone has an opinion about that tragedy and about school violence in general. When I feel that it is time to swing to the eternal, I just ask, "What do you think happened to those fifteen people when they walked off the planet?" Suddenly, you are having an eternal conversation, learning about what the person believes.

On a flight from Los Angeles to Atlanta, I was sitting next to a pilot who was hopping to another city to catch his next assignment. We were just talking casually, which is a good thing to do with people. It builds rapport and trust, so when you transition to the eternal they are more willing to listen. After a while, I asked the pilot what he thought about the Alaska Airlines plane that crashed a couple of years ago. The plane had had mechanical problems and plummeted into the Pacific Ocean, killing all eighty-eight onboard. He said passionately, "I am sick and tired of the fact that I have to trust those mechanics. If the mechanics don't do their job, I am at their mercy."

> *Didn't someone lead you to Jesus? If so, then you actually do know how to lead someone to the Lord.*

I could see where that would be stressful for a pilot. So I empathized with him as we talked for another few minutes about the circumstances of that crash. Then I asked, "By the way, what do you think happens when eighty-eight people walk off the planet like that?"

He told me that he believed in reincarnation. We talked the whole rest of the flight about reincarnation, Heaven and Hell, the truth of the Bible, etc.

Of course, now we have the September 11th attacks that we can use to begin a conversation. Everyone everywhere has an opinion about that event. Then simply ask people where they think those 3,000 victims are right now, and you will have an eternal conversation about what they believe.

The following chapters will help you learn how to share your faith with anyone. We'll look at additional ways to begin a conversation about eternal matters, what to actually say in witnessing, and how to counter arguments and answer questions. After reading this book, no one will be able to say that he doesn't know how to witness!

Fear of Losing a Friend
This is a primary reason cited by young people for why they don't share their faith. But what kind of friendship do you really have if you would go to Heaven when you die, but your friend would go to Hell? If you are friends for 20 years then separated for 800 million plus years, what kind of friendship is that? If you are not eternal friends, are you really friends at all?

Outside a rock concert, I was handing out tracts to people as they were going into the show. One guy, Ron, struck up a conversation with me. He said that he had read the tract and knew it was the truth. We talked awhile, but his friend, who looked like a rock star, didn't want anything to do with me, so they went into the concert. About thirty minutes later, Ron came walking up and said that he wanted to continue the conversation. He had asked the police officer to let him out of the concert so he could talk with me! He then said about his rock-star friend, "I think I am his friend just to reach him for God." God allows us to be friends with lost people so that we will plant seeds in their lives and help them to become eternal friends.

A few years ago, one of my high-school buddies told me over dinner, "You are the only friend I have who cares where my soul is going to spend eternity." What a great thing to hear from a friend! I am so glad I brought up the topic of eternity during that dinner. But if, in his words, I am the only person he knows who cares where he will spend eternity, trust me—God has placed me there for a specific reason: to be a vessel of His to be used in that person's life.

Read the following poem and let it sink into your soul.

My Friend

My friend, I stand in judgment now,
And feel that you're to blame somehow.
On Earth I walked with you day by day,
And never did you point the way.

You knew the Lord in truth and glory,
But never did you tell the story.
My knowledge then was very dim;
You could have led me safe to Him.

Though we lived together here on Earth,
You never told me of the second birth.
And now I stand this day condemned,
Because you failed to mention Him.

You taught me many things, that's true;
I called you "friend" and trusted you.
But I learn now that it's too late,
And you could have kept me from this fate.

We walked by day and talked by night,
And yet you showed me not the light.
You let me live, and love, and die,
You knew I'd never live on high.

Yes, I called you "friend" in life,
And trusted you through joy and strife.
And, yet, on coming to this dreadful end,
I cannot, now, call you "my friend."

Don't worry about losing friends by witnessing to them. When people see and hear the love of Jesus coming from you, you will have more friends than you know what to do with. I want to know tons of people in Heaven! That means I had better be inviting a whole lot of people to Heaven while I'm here.

One guy told me that he wanted to get serious about all of this Jesus stuff, but he really wanted to be "cool." I asked him, "Do you know what 'cool' is? Going to Heaven on the day you die—now that is 'cool.' Do you know what 'really cool' is? Going to Heaven when you die and bringing a whole lot of people with you. Now that is 'really cool.'" Make sure that you spend your life being "really cool"!

They Have Already Heard

It's important to keep in mind that repetition is very valuable in witnessing. I heard recently that it takes an average of 7.6 times for people to hear the Gospel before they commit their life to Jesus. And you don't know if your conversation with someone is going to be number 1, 5, .6, or 75! God could be sending you to follow up on what someone else has done in that person's life. The key is to be faithful. First Corinthians 3:6 says, "I have planted, Apollos watered; but God gave the increase." Some of us plant seeds, some water the seeds, but only God is able to make those seeds grow.

Have you considered that this might be the perfect time for an individual to hear the Gospel? Because of circumstances in that person's life, today might be the day that God sends you to have a conversation with that friend or stranger. The person may have heard it before, but timing is very important.

A few years ago, I was witnessing to a man in an Atlanta mall who told me, "You are the eighth person this year to talk to me about Jesus Christ." He had apparently been thinking a lot on the issue, and recalled exactly how many people he had chatted with about it.

One time I approached three guys at a mall in Dallas and asked them, "If you died tonight, are you 100-percent assured that you would go to Heaven?" All three gave me an immediate no as they turned to walk away. I quickly handed each one a tract, and they were gone. After they had walked away I wondered, *Lord, what was the point of that conversation?*

About thirty minutes later, one of them walked up to me and said, "About two minutes after you approached us, I stopped dead square in the mall and asked myself the question, 'If I died tonight in a car accident going down Emerson Road in Dallas, am I 100-percent assured that I would go to Heaven?' And my answer was 'no.' I began at that moment to pray to God."

After he prayed, he came and found me. We sat down and had a thirty-minute conversation. This happened in late January, and his New Year's resolution had been to leave the homosexual lifestyle. So we talked about how to repent of sin and to start living for God. You will be amazed at what God can do when you just faithfully plant seeds. What I initially thought was a waste of time turned out to be perfect timing in that young man's life.

I Am Just Lazy
Believe it or not, this is one of the reasons people give for not witnessing. How do you think God feels when we say we are lazy, while multitudes of people die and go to Hell every single day? As a Christian, what is more important than seeing those in your family, your school, your city, your state, your country, and your world coming to the saving knowledge of Jesus Christ?

Excuses, Excuses

Yet, according to Zondervan Church Source, 97 percent of church members have no involvement in any sort of evangelism. A survey by *Christianity Today* found that only 1 percent of their readership had witnessed to someone "recently." Does anything strike you as being wrong with this picture? This does not sound like the people I read about in the New Testament who had so much zeal that they were willing to die for our Lord.

Probably the reason most people don't share their faith is that they really don't have any faith to share. Charles Spurgeon said, "Have you no wish for others to be saved? Then you are not saved yourself. Be sure of that." Please let the Lord strike an evangelistic zeal in your heart. Being lukewarm is not of the Lord.

Samuel Chadwick (1860–1932) wrote, "Why does the church stay indoors? They have a theology that dwindled into a philosophy, in which there is no thrill of faith, no terror of doom and no concern for souls. Unbelief has put out the fires of passion, and worldliness garlands that altar of sacrifice with the tawdry glitter of unreality."

Please let the Lord strike an evangelistic zeal in your heart. Being lukewarm is not of the Lord.

If God gave you a thousand dollars every time you shared your faith in Jesus Christ, would you share your faith? Let's be honest: many of us would quit our day jobs and become full-time evangelists! Every one of us, including me, ought to repent of the fact that we would share Jesus for a measly dollar bill, instead of sharing Him because of the unconditional love that He has for each one of us. Would you be more zealous for money than for God? Would you deal with your laziness problem for the love of money when you won't deal with it for the love of God? We can't serve both God and mammon. We can never repay Jesus for what He did for us on the cross, but what a fantastic thank-you we can give Him each time we step out and share our faith in Him with the lost!

Friendship Evangelism
Many Christians want the lost to simply look at their lives and be able to see that they love Jesus. I suppose that means the lost will need to infer that they too should love Jesus. First John 2:6 says, "He that saith he abideth in Him ought himself also so to walk, even as He walked." No doubt about it—everyone who calls himself a believer must strive to walk like Jesus did. John 4 tells us that Jesus made the first move to talk to the woman at the well. So to walk like He did, we must be available to the Spirit of God to initiate conversations with people as we're out witnessing.

Also, if people are looking at you, whose life are you really sharing—yours or God's? They would not know why you are supposedly such a good person, so you would be sharing your life only. And once you say you are a Christian, non-believers will watch everything you do. They like to see Christians stumble. So when you talk bad about the coach who doesn't give you enough playing time, drop a curse word into the conversation, talk about others behind their backs, etc., the lost are listening. Are you sure you want to witness by your actions alone? I definitely don't want to do that, because sometimes my actions don't portray my Savior in a very good light.

I had the opportunity a couple of years ago to speak at a missions conference at Biola University in Los Angeles. It was a great time, with many folks challenged by the messages God had me deliver. One day during lunch, some students invited me to sit with them. After we chatted a while, one of the girls said, "Mark, I heard everything you said today, but I am just going to share my faith by my actions."

When people say that, I tell them, "Oh, you must be thinking of Romans 1:16, 'I am ashamed of the Gospel of Christ....'"

They usually respond, "But that isn't what the verse says." That's true—the verse actually states, "...I am *not* ashamed of the Gospel of Christ: for it is the power of God unto salvation to every one that believeth; to the Jew first, and also to the Greek." When we don't want to talk about our faith, it is usually because we are ashamed of what people might think of us. However, God commands us to stand for Him and never be ashamed of Jesus.

I asked each of those students how they got saved. Their answers were what I expected: "My parents led me to Jesus." "I heard about Him at a revival meeting and made a commitment." "I was at church one Sunday and surrendered my life to the Lord." "A friend led me to Christ."

I then said, "Each one of you has just admitted that you are now a Christian because someone verbally told you about Jesus. Yet you want to come up with a new way to share your faith where you don't have to use words?" Suddenly they all realized the importance of speaking boldly about what they believe.

In Romans 10:13–17 Paul tells us:

> For whosoever shall call upon the name of the Lord shall be saved. How then shall they call on him in whom they have not believed? and how shall they believe in him of whom they have not heard? and how shall they hear without a preacher? And how shall they preach, except they be sent? as it is written, How beautiful are the feet of them that preach the gospel of peace, and bring glad tidings of good things!

But they have not all obeyed the Gospel. For Esaias saith, "Lord, who hath believed our report?" So then faith cometh by hearing, and hearing by the word of God.

People believe when the good news is preached and the Spirit of God touches their hearts. So preach the Good News as God (through Paul) tells us to!

I Don't Know Enough
If knowing everything were a prerequisite for us to share our faith, none of us could ever witness. Interestingly, though, witnessing is one of the best ways that you will learn more about your faith. When you talk with lost people and can't answer their questions, it drives you to the Bible and other books to find answers. Also, your prayer life changes. As you meet hurting people and you want them to know the Comforter, you begin to pray more for others and not just for yourself.

You may think that you don't know enough to confidently witness, but consider this: you are saved and the people you witness to are lost; who knows more in every spiritual conversation? You always know more than a lost person does in any conversation. As a believer, you have the Holy Spirit living within you to help you understand God's Word (1 Corinthians 2:12). You can comprehend spiritual truths that a lost person can't.

I read about a man who memorized the entire New Testament. To me, that's an amazing feat, especially since, at times, I struggle with a single verse! Two years later, that man bowed his heart and gave his life to Jesus. He had memorized the New Testament before he was saved! If you had talked with him before he was born again, you might have thought that he knew more than you did, but that wouldn't be true. You *know* Jesus with your mind and heart, and he only knew *about* Jesus, with his mind.

They Won't Want To Talk About It

On most days when I witness, I encounter no more than one person who won't talk with me. Usually everyone I approach is interested in a conversation. In this crazy world we live in, the lost are really curious about what is going on and are trying to make sense of things. We will be able to help them by providing answers to many of their questions.

I can't tell you how many people have told me, "I usually don't discuss this topic, but you make me feel so comfortable talking about it." When you witness in a loving, Christlike way, people will be interested in what you have to say.

During a recent physical, I took time to begin an eternal conversation with the doctor. After we had talked for a short time, she said, "There are two subjects that I don't talk about with patients: religion and politics. But...since we have already started!" We had a great conversation. Always assume that people *do* want to talk about eternity, and not that they don't want to talk about it. Therefore, before you leave your house, it's important to pray that the Lord will lead you to lost people during the day, and that He will soften the individuals' hearts before you ever begin the conversations. That way, you know they'll be ready for you when you get there!

I Can't Answer Their Questions

This is a big stumbling block for many people. They worry that they might look foolish if they can't answer someone's questions. But listen to what God tells us in Psalm 14:1: "The fool hath said in his heart, 'There is no God.'" The fool is one who doesn't believe in God. You are not a fool just because you do not know an answer to a question.

ONE THING YOU CAN'T DO IN HEAVEN

If I don't know how to answer a question, I say something like, "That is a good question, and I don't know the answer. Would you like to know the answer?" People usually say "yes" because that's why they asked the question in the first place. So then I ask, "What is your e-mail, phone number, or address so when I find the answer, I can get it to you?" This allows me to follow up with people.

We should want to see people in Heaven so much that we would be willing to do anything for them to know Jesus.

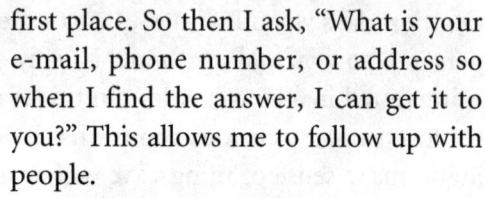

It really means a lot to people when believers actually follow up. It shows we care. I always try to get a business card from the individuals I talk with on a plane flight. I almost always send them a note, and sometimes a book. We should want to see people in Heaven so much that we would be willing to do anything for them to know Jesus.

In a later chapter, we will take a look at some of the questions you're likely to encounter when witnessing, and show you that they are really not that difficult to answer.

Now that you know there is no suitable excuse for not sharing your faith, let's look at a very easy way to begin planting those seeds of the Gospel—evangelistic tracts.

> But they cried out, "Away with him, away with him, crucify him." Pilate saith unto them, "Shall I crucify your King?"
> John 19:15

CHAPTER 5

DID YOU GET ONE OF THESE?

"When preaching and private talk are not available, you need to have a tract ready… Get good striking tracts, or none at all. But a touching gospel tract may be the seed of eternal life. Therefore, do not go out without your tracts."
CHARLES HADDON SPURGEON

A tract—a presentation of the Gospel on a small piece of paper, postcard, booklet, etc.—is one of the most important ways you can share your faith. Many lost people have a Bible but never read it, yet they will read something about Jesus that is not very long. Tracts are an effective way for the lost to hear Scripture, and are often used by God to give people an interest in reading His holy Word. They're a great way to plant seeds of the Gospel! Handing out tracts is also a very simple way to get started in witnessing. Shy people may want to begin by distributing tracts and then progress to verbal witnessing as their confidence builds.

When I am out witnessing using my survey approach (which I'll talk about in Chapter 7), I carry tracts in my pocket. As I get to the end of the conversation, I either read through the tract with the person or tell them, "I have a gift for you for helping me out." People love gifts—so give them a gift that talks about the greatest Gift ever given, Jesus Christ!

Tracts are useful even when you are verbally witnessing because you may get nervous and not say things the way you want to. A well-written tract will explain sin and the Gospel in a clear, concise manner.

Did You Get One of These?

One time in a mall, I approached a couple of teenage girls to begin a conversation. They didn't want to talk with me and turned to walk away. I said, "Well, you get a gift even though you didn't help me out." They came back, took two tracts from me, and began reading the tracts aloud to each other as they walked through the mall!

Another time, after I had been chatting with a couple of people for a few minutes, one of them said, "Wait a minute. You talked with me last year at this mall. Matter of fact, you gave me a booklet about Jesus, and I still know where it is."

I said in disbelief, "No, you don't."

"Yes, I do," he said. "It is on the top shelf of my desk right now." I was amazed that he knew right where it was, and I had the feeling he had read it more than once.

In Atlanta, a lot of concerts, basketball games, and other events are held at Philips Arena. I often hand out tracts to people as they come off the trains or are going into the arena. I will say something like, "Enjoy the game," or "Have a nice evening," and then extend a tract toward them. When you are friendly and smile, people usually respond the same way. So the nicer you are, the more likely they will talk with you or accept a tract from you. One day I was downtown at the arena handing out tracts, and a girl walked up and asked, "What have you got for me this time?"

She described each of the three tracts I had given her before, and she wanted to know if I had any new ones! She was not a believer, but she really liked the tracts. A couple of weeks after the September 11th attacks, I was downtown handing out tracts again. She approached me and started a conversation, and we talked for over an hour. But we would never have talked if I had not handed her a tract that first time.

When I go downtown, I often hand out tracts on one side of an arena or football stadium to the people attending the event. Then once the event starts, I go to the other side of the arena and put tracts on cars in the parking lot. Many times I will ask a homeless man to help me, and pay him for his time. You can place the tracts under windshield wipers, but a much better idea, if the tract is not flimsy, is to slide it between the rubber piece and the window by the driver's side door handle. That way the people see it when they unlock their doors and can easily grab it. Most people don't like to litter, so they will place the tract in their car and drive off. I have seen many individuals sit in their cars and read the entire tract before driving away. So be encouraged—the lost really do read them.

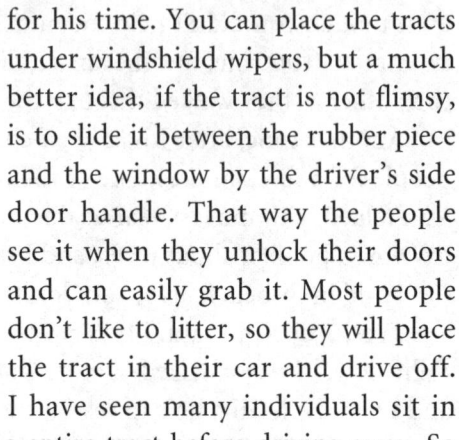

"Did you get one of these?" This is a great question that makes people feel like they are missing out on something. And they are.

As I walk through airports, I like to hand out tracts before boarding my plane. I ask people, "Did you get one of these?" They usually say that they didn't, and then take one. This is a great question that makes them feel like they are missing out on something. And they are. They are missing out on the best thing in this world and in the next one—Jesus Christ. Use this question, and you will hand out a lot of tracts!

The Value of a Soul

Beach areas are also great places to witness. Whether it is the daytime when people are worshiping the sun or nighttime when they worship the night life, people always seem to be hanging out and ready for conversations. One night in Myrtle Beach, South Carolina, I was out witnessing with a young man who had heard me speak at a camp. We were using the survey approach, and had an excellent twenty-minute conversation with three eighteen-year-old girls from Kentucky. At the end of the conversation, I told the young ladies that they got a gift for helping us out. I handed the first two a tract, but the third girl declined.

I asked, "After the great conversation we just had, you don't want this?"

She replied, "No, I don't."

"Okay," I said. "I'll give you a dollar to read it."

"Nope."

"Two dollars."

She shook her head.

"I'll give you five dollars to read it."

She still refused.

"I'll give you ten dollars to read it!" I persisted.

She finally agreed. So I put a ten-dollar bill with the tract and extended it toward her, then pulled it back slightly and said, "Now, anyone who would walk up to you and share his faith is assured that he has the right answer. And anyone who would pay you to read about his faith is 100-percent assured that he has the right answer!" I then handed her the money with the tract. You should have seen the surprised look on her face. I am pretty sure that no one had witnessed to her before, but I am convinced that no one had ever given her money to read about God. I don't think those girls will ever forget the conversation we had that night.

At the time I did that, a few years ago, I had just recently started public speaking and made about $4,000 that year. With an annual income of $4,000, $10 is very important. But do you think that, if you spend $10 for someone to read about Jesus, God will get $10 back into your pocket? You had better believe it! God is more faithful than we can ever dream. The great missionary Hudson Taylor said, "God's work done in God's way will never lack God's supplies." A few days later as I was praying, God really touched my spirit. It was very clear that He was asking me how much a soul was worth. Was it worth $10? $20? $4,000? And God clearly impressed my spirit that we should be willing to empty our bank accounts for one person to know Jesus Christ! We can't imagine the value of a soul to God except to look at the cross.

Think about this. Why are we the only generation in history that feels we need $300,000 in an IRA on which to retire? Why didn't any other generation feel that way? Are we trusting money more than we are trusting God to take care of our needs in life? I am not saying that we shouldn't plan for the future, but why does God allow some people to have that much money?

How will we feel on Judgment Day when God asks us what we plan to do with all that money now that we are dead—and then He explains that the income He blessed us with was intended to support missionaries, buy Bibles, and to help spread the Gospel to the ends of the earth? We will not feel good on that day.

A couple of years ago I had some money in an IRA. Although it was not a lot, it seemed like it to me. I finally realized why I had that money, and it was not to retire on. It was for me to fall back on just in case this whole speaking thing didn't work out! That is pretty shallow and not too godly, so God started to tug on my heart to take the money out and give it away. If you only knew how difficult this was for me! At the time, I was one of the stingiest people ever with a dollar bill. The decision was excruciating, but I knew what I needed to do. I took the money out of the IRA and began giving it away. I was supporting missionaries in other countries, buying Bibles for China and Sudan, feeding the hungry, etc. It was so much fun to give it all away!

Did You Get One of These?

A few months later, however, I had to pay my taxes. I had completely forgotten that I owed tax on the money I withdrew, and I had not set any of it aside to pay the taxes. But God, who knows all our needs, had someone give me enough money to cover the taxes! Through that experience, God has taught me to be a giver, and to really know what He means when He says that "it is more blessed to give than to receive" (Acts 20:35). Please be a giver. It is the only way to live this life.

There are few things I hate in life, but grocery shopping is one of them. Since I love to eat, however, it is one of those necessary evils. One time in a grocery store, I was next in line to check out. I could tell by their language that the family in front of me was from another country. They didn't look like they had a lot of money, so I had the thought that I should buy their groceries. While the cashier was checking their groceries, their son was checking out the interesting items on the racks. He reached down and picked up a huge squirt gun called a Supersoaker. His dad had him put it down because, obviously, he couldn't afford it. So I bought him a Supersoaker! He was so excited. When I checked my two items out, my bill was $79—and I just went in to get two items!

God has taught me to be a giver, and to really know what He means when He says that "it is more blessed to give than to receive."

Afterwards, I was chatting with the family and discovered there was only one person in the family who could speak English. Can you guess who it was? It was the young kid with a brand new Supersoaker!

So I shared the Gospel with him, gave him a tract, and asked him to share it with his parents. Keep doing crazy, loving things for our God. He can use your generosity to touch lives and make an eternal impact.

Give People a Surprise
One reason I hate to go to grocery stores is that I can't usually do as much witnessing there as I would like. So to make the most of the opportunities, I park at the far end of the parking lot and place tracts on the cars as I walk in. Then once inside, I walk over to the beer section and slide a small tract (two inches by three inches) inside twelve-packs and cases of beer. Then I head over to the twelve-packs of Coke and Pepsi. Those companies are so thoughtful they actually put a slit on the side of their cartons that is just perfect for sliding tracts into! I figure if Cracker Jacks can give people a surprise, why can't I?

One day, as I was walking out of a bank, I noticed three guys in a van. I walked over to them and began to hand them tracts. As I handed the third guy one of those small tracts, called a Smartcard, he said, "Oh, I've seen one of those!"

Surprised, I asked, "You've seen one of these?" I had just gotten there, so I couldn't figure out how he had seen one.

He said, "I bought an eighteen-pack of beer the other day, and that thing was slid right down inside there!"

Amazing! Just a few days after finding a tract in his beer, he met the guy who put it there. We serve a great God. Keep planting those seeds. He will give you creative ideas for reaching the lost.

Getting to my first speaking engagement in Canada proved to be quite an experience. The trip from Atlanta to Medicine Hat required three connections. I don't often get sick, but I was not feeling well this day. Once in Calgary, I needed a passport to get through customs. Unfortunately, I

Did You Get One of These?

didn't have mine with me, so I had to go through another line. Once through that line, I rushed to make my connection and arrived at the gate just as the door was closing for boarding. I tried all of my persuasive ability to get on that plane, but to no avail. I had to wait another two hours for the next flight, and I was none too happy!

While I was sulking, I decided to walk around the airport and hand out tracts. I stopped to look around a gift shop, then I handed the man behind the counter a tract as I left. A while later I was walking down the same hallway, and that man saw me. He called me over to talk, and told me that he was a Christian and his father was the airport chaplain. Because not all chaplains are followers of Jesus, I first did some probing to make sure this man really had made a commitment to Christ.

He said, "Yesterday, my dad tapped the pocket on my shirt and told me, 'That is a tract pocket.'" His dad meant that it was a pocket to hold tracts so that he could give them away. "I didn't know what a tract was," he continued. "Now I do, since you handed me one, and now I know where to get them!" When you're running late, thank God and see how He might use you to glorify Him and further His kingdom.

After I spoke at a Christian school in Augusta, Georgia, one of the teachers took me out for dinner. We drove to downtown Augusta, parked the car, and began to walk toward the restaurant. I noticed a woman by a car, so I walked over and asked her, "Did you get one of these?"

She said, "No." I handed her a tract, told her to have a good evening, and continued toward the restaurant.

As we were sitting in the restaurant getting ready to order, the teacher looked up and said, "Mark, it's time for some follow-up."

I said, "Follow-up? I haven't done any witnessing yet."

He pointed toward the door as that woman walked into the restaurant. How she found us I will never know; the restaurant we were in was a good stretch away from where I had handed her the tract. She came over to our table, held out the tract and asked, "Did you give me this?"

I responded, "Yes, I did."

She said, "You don't know how much I needed to hear what this had to say." I reached out and took her hand, and shared with her what the Lord had done in my life, and what He could do in her life.

She continued, "My roommate is my rock. She is a Christian. She's a waitress in a local restaurant, but she used to be a dancer just like I am." This woman was a stripper in a local strip joint! Pointing to the tract, she said, "This is now the third thing that God has done to let me know the exact decision that I need to make, and this is the icing on the cake!"

If God can use a five-cent piece of paper in that woman's life, He can use it in anyone's life.

Tears were welling up in her eyes, so I asked her if I could give her a hug. As I stood up and began to bend over to hug her, I noticed that several people in the restaurant were watching us. With her short shorts and a windbreaker over her top, this woman didn't fit the atmosphere.

What were all those people thinking? They may have thought that I was getting a special favor for giving her a good tip at the club where she worked! Little did they know that I got the chance to see eternity touch this lady's heart—all because of a five-cent piece of paper. I didn't care what those people thought; their opinions didn't matter. What matters is that we step out in faith and let the Lord use us. If God can use a five-cent piece of paper in that woman's life,

Did You Get One of These?

He can use it in anyone's life. Just step out in faith, and let the Lord use you as a vessel to bring eternity, salvation, and surrender to the lost. With tracts, it couldn't be easier.

As Spurgeon said, we need "good striking tracts" when we witness. My favorite tracts come from Living Waters Publications. You can contact them at www.livingwaters.com or at 800-437-1893. Chick Publications also makes good tracts. You can view their tracts at www.chick.com.

When I started sharing my faith, I never used tracts. I learned how to witness by having a verbal conversation with a lost person. To this day the most thrilling part of witnessing is a good conversation with someone who doesn't know Jesus.

The following chapters will give you the tools necessary to have those conversations with everyone you meet.

*And they compel one Simon a Cyrenian…
to bear his cross.*
Mark 15:21

CHAPTER 6

IF THEY'RE BREATHING, THEY NEED JESUS

"To be a soul winner is the happiest thing in the world. And with every soul you bring to Jesus Christ, you seem to get a new heaven here upon earth."
CHARLES HADDON SPURGEON

Former Beatle George Harrison said in an interview, "There is nothing more important than finding out what is after death. What happens to us after we die?" It was Harrison's faith, the interviewer stated, that got him through his battle with cancer. One of his big solo hits was "My Sweet Lord." The only problem was that Harrison was not a Christian; his lord was a Hindu god! Although his faith may have helped him through his illness, it will not help him on Judgment Day.

As believers, we know what happens to us after we die. Second Corinthians 5:8 says, "We are confident, I say, and willing rather to be absent from the body, and to be present with the Lord." The only true Lord, of course, is Jesus Christ.

As we talk with people, how can we get them to think about what happens after death? I am a firm believer that before someone can accept Jesus, he must be thinking about his eternal destination. So let's look at some ways we can help people to consider—and continue to think about—eternal matters.

Tombstone example

One way to get people to consider eternity is to ask them to identify the three basic items found on a tombstone. The answers are the deceased person's name, date of birth, and date of death.

Then say, "I can make you a guarantee. I guarantee that you will be dead a whole lot longer than you will be alive. Since that's true, you should be searching out what is on the other side instead of searching out things down here that are temporary, because you will be there a whole lot longer than you will be here on earth."

Dwight Moody, the great preacher, said that if he could get someone to think about eternity for five minutes, he could lead the person to Jesus Christ. I believe that one of Satan's best tricks is to get people to focus on college, jobs, family, retirement, bank accounts, etc., and avoid thinking about eternity. We must help people begin to consider what will happen to them when they die.

150 years from now...

Ask someone, "A hundred and fifty years from now, will it matter if you made a million dollars, drove a convertible Mercedes, graduated from college, played in the Final Four? No. The only thing that will be important then is whether you know the God who created you, because you will be in one of two destinations forever...and ever and ever." It is very important to get people to realize that it is the eternal, not temporary, things that matter.

What then?

One day I was talking with a seventeen-year-old who

worked at the mall. We were chatting about life, so I asked him what he was going to do after high school.

He said, "I've been looking at some colleges, and probably will go to college."

I asked, "What then?"

"Well," he answered, "after I graduate from college, I'll probably get a job."

"What then?"

"I will probably get married and have some kids."

"What then?"

"I guess I will retire."

I continued, "What then?"

"I guess I will die."

"What then?"

"Now that's a good question," he said.

That *is* a good question, one that everyone will have to answer one day. He didn't have an answer at that point, but he knew what the answer was before our conversation ended. This "what then" approach is a very simple, conversational way to talk with someone about eternity.

Eternity is an awfully long time. Make sure you've got the right answer.

On an airplane flight, I had a brief conversation with a man across the aisle. It didn't go very well in an earthly sense. I handed him a tract, which he read and handed back. He was an atheist and didn't want anything to do with me.

As we stood to leave the plane, I tried to say a couple of encouraging things to him. Then added, "Remember, eternity is an awfully long time; make sure you've got the right answer."

I could see in his eyes that that thought made an impact. He had never considered how long eternity was. Now he had to.

As I was talking with a student at the University of Georgia, I asked him why he was in college. He said, "It's what you do after high school."

I said, "No, why are *you* here?"

"To get a degree."

I persisted, "No, why are you *really* here?"

"So I can do something with my life," he replied.

Ten out of ten people die. Don't be afraid to remind people of that.

"Exactly," I said. "You want to do something in this journey that we call life. Job 16:22 says, 'When a few years are come, then I shall go the way whence I shall not return.' If you are going to study and search to make sure you do something with your life, why wouldn't you study and search about the journey into eternity that every one of us must take?"

The light went on. He knew he was going to die, and he knew eternity was a long time, so he would be smart to find out what would be waiting for him.

There is a 100-percent chance that you will die.
As I was talking with one man I asked, "Do you realize that there is a 100-percent chance that you will die?" Then I added, "And do you realize that you will be dead a whole lot longer than you will be alive?" This gentleman looked at me and said, "Say that again." Those two statements made him think so much that he wanted me to repeat them! Ten out of ten people die. Don't be afraid to remind people of that.

Can you guarantee that you will wake up tomorrow morning? Don't put your head on your pillow tonight unless you know exactly where you are going to spend eternity.
While I was chatting with three people at a popular arts

festival, I noticed a young man who sat down about ten feet away and was watching us. When I finished talking with this group several minutes later, the young man was still there. So I walked over and asked if I could help him. He said, "Do you remember me? You talked with me and several of my friends at Piedmont Park a few months ago."

At that festival, I had sat down with a group of teenagers and had a conversation with them. It didn't go very well in my opinion. Now, three months later, this seventeen-year-old recognized me and wanted to talk.

I asked him about the conversation we had then, and he relayed our conversation almost word-for-word the way I witness.

I then asked, "What do you remember most about the conversation?"

He replied, "The very last thing you said. You asked me, can I guarantee that I will wake up tomorrow morning? I think about it every single day that I wake up!"

His first thought in the morning is about where he would be if he had not woken up. God was working on this young man's heart!

A couple of days later as I was praying, wondering how this young man could have remembered all this after three months, God spoke to my heart with a still, small voice. He said, "When you plant a seed, I will do something with it!" Our God is so faithful; He takes the meager seeds that we plant and makes them grow (1 Corinthians 3:7). Keep planting those seeds!

BIBLE: Basic Information Before Leaving Earth

This is a great acronym that people really like—and one they remember. I explain that it doesn't matter who you are—Michael Jordan, the president, you, or me—we will all be leaving earth one day. If you have the right information about eternity and do something with it, you will end up at the right destination; but if you have the wrong information, you will end up at the wrong destination!

I once wrote this acronym on the back of a tract that I gave someone. The guy looked at it and said, "Wow." Then he repeated, "Wow!" It really made him think. Use it sometime and observe the person's reaction.

I care where you spend eternity. *(or)* **It is very important to me where you spend eternity.**

If you can look someone in the eyes and say this and *mean* it, it will have a tremendous impact. Many people care about others in a temporal sense, but few care in an eternal sense. When you show people that you care about their eternal well-being, they will gladly listen to you when you talk about spiritual truth.

After speaking at the Citadel, a military college in Charleston, South Carolina, I went with a few of the cadets to the bar section of town to witness. One of the cadets stopped to talk to a man sitting outside a bar. As they were talking, the guy asked the cadet, "What are you doing out here?"

The cadet said, "I am just out here meeting people and talking with them."

The other guy insisted, "No, what are you really doing out here?"

"I am a believer in Jesus Christ," he replied. "And because I love God, that means I love you, and I care where you will spend eternity. I want to see you in Heaven one day."

It so impacted the guy that he stood up, grabbed the cadet (he was a huge cadet in full dress uniform), and gave him a hug. Twenty minutes later that guy bowed his heart and committed his life to the God of this universe.

I called one of my buddies, Doug, on his birthday. He is a young man who has been through a lot, and is not always heading in the right direction. But he is one of those people I really love and want to see in Heaven one day. So after I went through several of the questions mentioned in this book, I told Doug, "I share all this with you because it is very important to me where you are going to spend eternity, and, Doug, I hope that means something to you."

With heartfelt emotion Doug replied, "It does. It really does." When people know that we care, they will listen when we share.

Make a friend, be a friend, lead a friend to Christ!

Studies have shown that 87 percent of all people who come to Jesus were introduced through a friend. We need to be about the business of making friends who do not know Jesus. This isn't so they can pull us away from Jesus, but so the Lord can use us to draw them to Him.

Personally, I don't have time for temporary friendships (that is, just hanging out with people who don't know the Lord). I do have a lot of temporary friends, but it's for the purpose of making them eternal friends. And it isn't that I talk about Jesus twenty-four hours a day. Although I would like to, I don't because it would push them away. I have them as friends for the express purpose of loving them like Jesus would, talking to them about Jesus as I have opportunity, and eventually seeing them in Heaven for all of eternity.

By the way, Ephesians 4:15 reminds us that we should be "speaking the truth in love." When you share your faith, if you are going to shove it down someone's throat, the best advice I can give you is to keep your faith to yourself. We don't need to *shove* it on someone, but to *love* it on someone.

One Thing You Can't Do in Heaven

The best lovers on earth should be Christians. Our Bible says that "God is love" (1 John 4:8), and we have a relationship with Him. Don't let anyone out-love you, but let the love of God shine through you.

The Budweiser ads say a real friend doesn't let a friend drive drunk. At Auburn University, we always said that a real friend doesn't let a friend go to Alabama! And the God of this universe says: *A real friend doesn't let a friend go to Hell. A real friend tells a friend about Jesus!*

If you want to see your friends in Heaven, invite them. If you don't want to see your friends in Heaven, don't invite them.

It is very simple. If you want to see your friends in Heaven, invite them. If you don't want to see your friends in Heaven, don't invite them. Remember: It is our responsibility to invite others to Heaven with us; it is their responsibility to decide how to respond to the invitation. They can throw it in the trash or they can take it and cash it in, but it is our job to issue the invitation.

Basketball has been a major part of my life. As I mentioned earlier, I played college basketball at Auburn University in the Southeastern Conference. Charles Barkley was at Auburn during three of my four years there, and we became pretty good friends, often rooming together on road trips. We have stayed in touch through the years, which has been a lot of fun.

One time I was visiting him in Birmingham, Alabama, and six of us went out for lunch. While we were sitting in the restaurant, I threw out a spiritual question for the whole table.

The next thing I knew, the entire group was talking about eternal things.

Charles pointed at me from across the table and said, "Mark is the only friend I have who is into this whole God and religion thing."

How does Charles know I am into that? I talk about it. I don't talk about it all the time with Charles, but I do talk about it. Why? I want to see Charles in Heaven. And because I do, I had better invite him!

Charles is a big man; he could break me in half any time he wanted to. Once he actually picked me up and threw me over his shoulder, and I'm a pretty decent-sized guy myself! But he appreciates the fact that I bring up that topic because he knows it takes guts to talk about it.

Did you notice, though, that he said I'm the *only* friend he has who is into religion? It might be that you are the only Christian friend of someone who is lost, and God has strategically placed you in that person's life for a purpose. The question is, what are you going to do about it? You are there to plant a seed in that person's life, so go for it. You will not regret it. I never regret bringing up the topic of God with people. The only regret I have is when I don't bring it up.

As Charles and I were hitting golf balls later that day, we talked again about eternal things. At one point I said, "I have to be honest. This is the most open I have seen you to the topic of God and Jesus Christ."

Charles responded, "Mark, when you get a little bit older and your career starts winding down, you begin to think about these things." Remember, in the life of the person God wants you to witness to, it might just be the perfect time for you to have that conversation.

Charles and I went back to his mother's house and were in the kitchen with his younger brother, Darryl. When Charles went to another room, Darryl told me, "You know, I had a heart attack a couple of months ago."

Then he added, "I saw something."

You have probably heard about near-death experiences, where some people who briefly died reportedly saw a tunnel and a white light. But many people see other things, and Darryl did not have the typical experience. He told me that when his heart stopped, his spirit rose up out of his body, and he could look down and see his body on the operating table. He explained that his spirit took off on a journey. Suddenly he saw trees burning, the ground smoldering around the trees, and a lake of fire in front of him. I asked, "What did you see?"

"I saw Hell."

"You saw Hell? Darryl, if you would have died, where would you have gone?"

He said confidently, "I would have gone to Hell."

"Do you want to go to Hell?"

He responded, "Absolutely not."

"Do you want to go to Heaven?"

"Yes, I do."

"Darryl," I prompted, "do you know what it takes to get to Heaven?"

"Yes, I do."

"What does it take?"

He stated, "Committing my heart and my life to Jesus Christ."

"Darryl, now that you know that you are going to die and go to Hell, are you ready to commit your heart and your life to Jesus Christ?"

What do you think he said? He answered, "No."

I asked, "Why not?"

He gave the same answer most people give: "I like the things of the world more than I like the things of God." He would rather live in sin than live for the God of this universe.

I tried to stress the seriousness of his decision by asking, "Do you realize that you will have no excuse when you stand in front of God on Judgment Day?"

"Yes," he replied, "I know."

That was one of the saddest conversations I have ever had. He knows what he needs to do to avoid an eternity in Hell, but the cares of the world are more important at this point in his life. He told me that what he saw was no dream, but was the most vivid, real thing he has ever seen. It was more real than the book you are reading or the chair on which you are sitting.

As he told me the story, I watched his eyes growing larger as he relived that experience. Believe it or not, his story is just one of many I have heard from people who have seen Hell instead of a tunnel and white light. Some have reported seeing people standing in pits of fire, their skin melting off their bodies, then coming back on and melting off again. These stories sound amazing, but our Bible does tell us about a lake of fire for those who experience the second death.

I have a question for you. If one of your friends died today, would they see a lake of fire for eternity? If you are like most people, your answer would be "yes." The question now is, what are you going to do about it? Are you really going to let your friends die and go to Hell for all of eternity? You can't let them go there. Jesus did His part two thousand years ago, and now it is time for you to do yours. Have that conversation with them, or write that letter, and you and God and *they* will be glad you did!

Michael Jordan's soul
When I was speaking at a conference in Phoenix, Arizona, where Charles lives, I called him to see if we could get

together. He asked, "Why don't you hang out with us tonight?" Charles tends to stay out late, and I had to speak that night and the next morning. But before I declined I asked,

"Us? Who is in town?"

He replied, "Michael Jordan is in town."

I was thinking, *I'm sure we can work this out!* I admit to being shallow at times, and this would be one of those moments. So what if I was a little tired the next day? I didn't want to pass up the opportunity!

After my speaking engagement that night, I met Charles and Michael at a cigar bar. Charles and his friends were sitting in the back on couches and chairs, surrounded by security people so no one would bother them. While I was there, the Lord impressed me that I should witness to the guy next to me.

Because he wasn't one of the famous people, I thought, *I don't want to talk to him—I want to talk to HIM (Michael Jordan)!* God prompted my spirit again to talk with the guy next to me. As I was praying a few days later, God just drilled me. I hate when He does that, but He only does it because He loves us and is trying to mold us into the people He called us to be. God laid on my heart, "Mark, was that soul next to you any less important to me than Michael Jordan's soul?"

Jesus did His part two thousand years ago, and now it is time for you to do yours.

Oh, my goodness! I realized that I had gone to that place to get a story. During the conference, I had told the attendees that I was going to witness to Michael Jordan that night. This would be the third time that I would be able to hang out with him and Charles, but I had never been bold enough to talk to him about Jesus. We talked about other things, but not about eternity. How sad to think that I didn't go there that night just to be used by God, but to get a story. Isn't it great that we serve the God of second chances? Remember, every soul is valuable to God. His Son is the price tag for every single soul.

As I sat next to this guy, I chatted with him briefly, then transitioned to the eternal. We had a good talk. He'd become a believer about five months earlier and was in a real growth phase of his Christian walk. He asked me a very interesting question: "What do you suppose God would think about us hanging out in a place like this?" We were in a place where people drank, smoked cigars, and danced; it was not a godly place.

I told him that I thought God would be concerned about only one thing: our motive for being there. "If you came here to just hang out with these famous people," I said, "you have wasted a good evening. I came here for a specific reason. There is someone in this club to talk to about Jesus Christ." Why else would Satan have bars? They draw lost people together so we can witness to them! We had a very encouraging conversation.

When the lights came on in the club at 1 a.m., Charles informed me that it was closing time. He loves staying out late, so I couldn't believe he would live in a place where all the clubs close that early. But Phoenix has a lot of good golf courses, and Charles loves to play golf! The owner came over and told Charles that he and his friends could stay after everyone else left.

That's when the party started. The owner brought Charles a case of the beer he had been drinking, and Michael Jordan went up to the bar and was downing shots of tequila. Please understand that what you see of celebrities on TV is often not what they are like in real life. Commercials will tell you to "be like Mike."

This is why it is important *not* to be like Mike, but to be like Jesus in all that you do.

Michael came over to where we were sitting and poured a large shot of tequila for Charles. Charles was shaking his head like he didn't want to do it. I gave him a look that said "don't do it." Michael was egging him on to do it. So he did it. The look on his face afterward said that he probably shouldn't have done that shot. It is amazing how our pride can get in the way of doing the right thing.

Next the bartender poured a shot for a girl sitting next to me. She drank it, and the look on her face said she shouldn't have done it either. Then the bartender poured a shot and handed it toward me. This was absolutely no temptation for me. I used to drink, but when you give something totally over to God, He can completely remove the desire for it. So I put out my hand and said, "I don't drink."

Suddenly Charles put his hand in front of mine, looked at the bartender and said, "Hey man, he doesn't drink."

Remember this, folks. Some of you have made your stand that you are not going to drink, use drugs, have immoral sex, etc. Don't back down. Because when push comes to shove, many times it is non-believers who will stand up for you quicker than believers will. They respect the position you have taken, although they may not say so.

So don't back down; make your stand and stand strong. The bartender then took the shot and drank it himself! It was a crazy night.

A few minutes later, Michael announced it was time to go. As we were walking out to our cars, Michael was just a couple of steps in front of me. I was praying for God to turn this guy around so I could talk with him. That's the reason I went there that night. I was thinking, *God, what do I have to do, slap his big bald head and say, "Turn around!"*?

Then, just as he got to his car, he turned around! So I decided to approach him. Do you think I was nervous at this point? You bet I was! Remember, we get nervous sometimes when we share our faith, but that shouldn't stop us. We have the only right answer for eternity and we cannot keep it to ourselves. We must tell the world about Jesus.

As I was approaching Michael, Charles walked over. He said, "Michael, don't forget that this is a buddy of mine from college." I was too nervous to figure out what Charles was doing, but as I thought about it later, I think Charles knew that I was going to witness to Michael, and in guy lingo he was telling Michael not to be a jerk to me because I was a friend.

As I reached out to shake Michael's hand, I realized that we were exactly the same size. And all that came to my mind was, *We are the same size, but you jump so much higher than I do!* Then I thought, *Cut it out—you have to start witnessing!* So I said, "Michael, I am here speaking at a conference, and I just wanted to ask you a question."

It doesn't matter whether people like us. Jesus was perfect, loved everyone perfectly, and still got nailed to a cross!

He replied, "Okay."

I asked, "Michael, when you die, what do you think is on the other side? What do you think is out there when we walk out of here?" A serious look came into his eyes, and he started nodding his head and thinking. There was a ten-second silence, which is a long time for silence in a conversation. (I call it eternity plus!) But when people are being silent and thinking, don't say anything; let the Lord work on them.

Michael finally answered, "I think there are those pearly gates when we die."

One Thing You Can't Do in Heaven

I knew I didn't have much time, so I asked this question: "Michael, have you ever committed your heart and life to Jesus Christ?" (I wish I would have said something else, but that is how it goes sometimes.) And quicker than that man jumps off the floor, he answered, "Yes, I have." But even quicker he added, "Have you talked to Charles about this?"

I said, "Yes, we talked about it a few months ago." Michael just shook his head and began to walk away. So I handed him a tract, and that was it.

Because Charles used valet parking, and I parked in the "cheap seats," Charles was going to give me a ride to my car. As I crawled into the back seat of his car, sitting on one side of me was Quinn Buckner, who played basketball at Indiana University and was a former head coach of the Dallas Mavericks. On the other side was Alex Rodriguez, who used to be the shortstop for the Seattle Mariners and was now with the Texas Rangers.

Even though it didn't go as well as I'd hoped, I had just witnessed to Michael Jordan, and I was on cloud nine, ten, and eleven all at the same time! So I asked Alex, "Can I ask you a question?" The next thing you know, I am talking about eternity with Alex and Quinn. When we got to my car, I handed them some tracts and hopped out of the car. Charles walked me to my car, and invited me over for dinner the following night before I had to leave for a speaking engagement in Tucson.

The next night when I went to Charles' house, who should I see but Michael Jordan! I walked into the area where he was, he glanced at me, and then looked away, like he didn't want to even acknowledge my presence. By the way, is that okay? Yes, it is. The only thing Michael knows about me is that I love Jesus enough to try to tell him about Him; he basically couldn't handle a conversation on the topic of God.

Sometimes we get so worried that if we stand up for Jesus, people are not going to like us. The point is, it doesn't matter whether they like us. It matters whether we are living a life pleasing to the Lord. Jesus was perfect, loved everyone perfectly, and still got nailed to a cross! So I went over and said "hello" to Michael and asked how his day of golf went.

Later that night, Charles, Michael, and some friends were sitting at his kitchen table, drinking beer, smoking cigars, and playing blackjack. It was just a fun game between friends with some money being wagered. At one point in the game, Charles lost three straight hands to Michael, losing $4,000 in ten minutes! When I first got started in the speaking business, I made that much in a year!

From my safe spot on the couch, I observed, "Charles, that's a lot of money you just lost."

"It's okay, Mark," he replied. "I won $5,000 last night!"

The night before they had played cards on Michael's private jet while they flew in from Houston. It was like Monopoly money to these guys.

But as I watched them, their eyes seemed so empty. The money, cigars, and beer could not satisfy them. Nothing in life can satisfy us, except completely living wholeheartedly for Jesus.

As I was sitting on the couch, I decided to talk with a woman seated near me. She was from Chicago, where she had met Michael, but was now living in Phoenix. I learned that she had made a commitment to Jesus about five months earlier. She seemed very solid in her beliefs. So I told her that the night before, I had gotten into a spiritual conversation with Michael, but he wasn't interested in it.

She explained, "Ever since his dad died, Michael avoids conversation about Jesus." What do you think Michael could be thinking? He may be angry or bitter with God because of the death of his dad. That is understandable to a point. She also said that Michael used to talk with Horace Grant from the Bulls about religion, but doesn't have much to do with it now. I'm glad that I witnessed to Michael Jordan that night. I now pray for him more than ever before. When you begin to share your faith, your prayer life will change. Your prayers will begin to be for the lost, people whom you would never have met if you weren't out witnessing.

The Finality of Death

When I was teaching eighth and ninth grade at a Christian school, I would read the paper each morning to keep up with the news as well as to get bonus questions for my tests. It was a way to encourage my students to read the paper and be familiar with world events.

One morning I had finished the front page and the business section, and was reading the sports section. (I always save the sports section for last because it is the icing on the cake!) At the end of the sports section was an obituary page, and for some reason that morning I decided to read it. While most of those listed were older, I noticed there were also some young people who had died.

At that moment, I felt the Lord very clearly speaking to my heart. I did not hear a voice, but it was as clear in my spirit as the "winning, winning, winning" concept that God had revealed to me. God laid on my heart, "All these people died yesterday. All these people took their last breath yesterday. And, Mark, there is nothing you can do about it. You can't plant one more seed. You can't have one more conversation with any of them. Each of these people is in Heaven or Hell, and they will be there forever and ever and ever." I was stunned. The finality of what I'd read on the obituary page had never really hit me.

If They're Breathing, They Need Jesus

My heart was racing as I got dressed and drove to school. My first period that day was a ninth-grade Bible class. I told the students what had happened that morning and we talked about it as a group. We decided that once you read a friend's name on the obituary page, once you are at a friend's funeral it is too late to find out the most important piece of information about him: whether he knows Jesus Christ as his Savior. So we came up with a motto, one that I live my life by: If they're breathing, they need Jesus!

Think about it. Every breathing person you will ever meet needs Jesus. Those who are believers already realize how much they need Him in their life. Those who are non-believers most definitely need Him, for the rest of this life and for the eternal life to come. Since all these breathing people need Jesus, and you know Him personally (you *know* what I am going to say), just go ahead and tell everyone you meet about the Son of God until you draw your last breath!

By the way, do you realize that the God of this universe literally holds your breath in His palm? Daniel wrote about "the God in whose hand thy breath is, and whose are all thy ways" (Daniel 5:23). Why not thank God for giving you the breath of life today? And then use the breath that He has given you to further His kingdom here on earth until He returns.

> *Use the breath that He has given you to further His kingdom here on earth until He returns.*

And when they were come unto a place called Golgotha . . . a place of a skull . . .
Matthew 27:33

CHAPTER 7

SAY WHAT?

"If sinners will be damned, at least let them leap to Hell over our bodies. And if they will perish, let them perish with our arms about their knees, imploring them to stay. If Hell must be filled, at least let it be filled in the teeth of our exertions, and let not one go there unwarned or unprayed for."
CHARLES HADDON SPURGEON

The number-one reason people don't share their faith is that they are afraid of being rejected. That excuse has been eliminated by the Scriptures—now we know that every time we share our faith it is a winning situation. The next-biggest reason people don't share their faith is that they don't know how to.

As already pointed out, if someone has led you to Christ, then you know how to lead someone else to Christ. So, now that you've overcome those barriers and decided to step out and witness, let's say you've gotten someone thinking about matters of eternity. How do you transition to the Gospel?

Let's walk through some questions you can ask to learn about the person's spiritual beliefs. A conversation starter can be as simple as asking, "Do you believe in Easter (or Christmas)? What do you believe about it?" You can also ask for directions. I will approach someone at a gas station (or anywhere else) and say, "I need some directions. Can you help me out?" People always answer, "Sure, where are you trying to go?" "I am trying to get to Heaven," I respond. "Do you know how to get there?"

If the person says "yes," find out why. If he says "no," ask if he would like to know the way, or ask what he believes will happen after he dies. This question usually gets a great reaction; watch the person's expression when you ask for directions to Heaven!

Another good way to transition to a spiritual topic is to say, "Can I ask you an interesting question?" Or, "Can I ask you a tough question?" This helps to pique curiosity and get people thinking before you even ask the main question. Then simply ask any of the following questions to help you learn their spiritual beliefs.

Where are you on your spiritual journey? *(or)* What is happening spiritually in your life?

Everyone is on a spiritual journey of some sort, but the question is, what will be the final destination of that journey? Carl Sagan, a renowned atheist, was on a spiritual journey during his life. Now that he is dead, he is 100-percent assured of what is out there—but it's too late for him to do anything about it. We want to ensure that people know what is awaiting them *before* they leave the planet.

As I was on a flight from Los Angeles to Atlanta, a large man with scraggly hair sat down next to me. And I didn't say a word to him! I am normally very friendly, so I don't know why I did that. He quickly fell asleep. I witness to a lot of people, but even I won't witness to someone who is sleeping!

I was very tired myself because I had just flown in from Hong Kong after a mission trip in China, so I walked around on the plane a bit to keep myself awake.

I knew I was supposed to talk with the man seated next to me, so I prayed, "Lord, if You want me to talk with this guy, You must wake him up." Not five minutes after I sat back down, it was like he had had two cups of coffee, and he was awake and ready to go!

As we began to talk, I found him to be a very interesting man. He was a cameraman who worked for MTV. He had been a cameraman for VH1, the Super Bowl, etc., so he must be great at his job. By the way, comfort and strengthen a lost person whenever you get the chance. The Bible says that believers need this encouragement (1 Thessalonians 5:11, "Wherefore comfort yourselves together, and edify one another…"), and if we do, then surely lost people need it.

I took time to encourage him, then I said, "Can I ask you an interesting question? What is happening spiritually in your life?"

He responded, "Well, not much of anything."

I was thinking, *You have to give me more information than that!* So I followed up with, "Aren't all of us on a spiritual journey of some sort?"

He then added, "Well, when I visit my mother in New York, she takes me to church every Sunday."

Bingo! That was my opening, and we spent the rest of the flight talking about spiritual things, God, and Jesus. You can see why that is a great question.

Another benefit of that question is that it doesn't mention Jesus. It's a very powerful name, and if you mention it too early in a conversation, it can scare people off. It's important to build trust and friendship at the beginning of a conversation.

If you died tonight, are you 100-percent sure that you would go to Heaven?

I heard about a man in Australia who would walk up to someone and say, "Excuse me. If you died tonight, are you 100-

percent assured that you would go to Heaven?" And then he would hand the person a Gospel tract. That's all he said. He would try to do this to ten people each day, and he kept at it for forty years! Now that is faithfulness. At the end of those forty years, he had not heard of one piece of fruit from his ministry. When a pastor discovered several people who were saved because of seeds this man had planted, he investigated and found that the number of saved people reached into the tens of thousands! That is how powerful this question is. It gets right to the point and makes people think.

Is it possible that the people you talk with could die today? The answer is "yes." The only question is: Where will they be if they did die today? One day I was talking with one of my students in my office. I wanted to invest more time in him, so I asked if he would like to go out to dinner the next week. He said, "Mr. Cahill, I would love that." Little did I know that six hours later he would put a loaded pistol to his head and pull the trigger. I had only six hours left with this student, not a week.

People have told me that God had tugged on their heart to witness to someone and they didn't, and the person died the same day. I didn't feel impressed to witness to this student on that day; I had talked with him before about his salvation. Yet I wonder if I missed God's agenda that day because I already had my own. Keep listening for the still, small voice of the Lord so you will not have any regrets on Judgment Day.

A great way to start a conversation with a stranger is to use a survey approach. The word "survey" has a negative connotation so I often call it a "project." You can create you own survey questions and have your youth group or Bible study group talk with a certain number of people each week.

Say What?

Instead of using a large clipboard, which can be intimidating to the people I'm trying to talk with, I use a Post-It Note pad to record their responses. That also allows me to give them information, such as the title of a book I'd like them to read. Some believers using this approach carry 3"×5" cards or a small spiral notebook.

This particular question is a good one to use for a survey, because people answer it! One time I walked up to a gentleman in a mall and said, "Can you help me out? I'm working on a project." He didn't say a word!

I continued, "Well, I am asking people the question: If you died tonight, are you 100-percent sure that you would go to Heaven?"

He turned to me and responded, "You've asked the wrong man that question."

This is not how I wanted it to go. So I asked, "Why is that?"

He answered, "Because I am an atheist. When you die, you die, and that's all there is."

Forty-five minutes later, we were still talking! It's easy to talk to atheists about God; they have no way to defend their position. They cannot prove that there is no God. The man told me that a few years earlier his closest buddy committed his life to Jesus, and then died in a car accident two weeks later! We had a marvelous talk. He then asked me if that survey was just to allow me to talk about Jesus.

"I use the data for talks that I give," I replied, "but basically, yes, that is what it is for."

He said, "That's a great idea!" Numerous lost people have mentioned that the survey approach is a good idea.

By the way, can believers in Jesus be 100-percent sure that if they died today they would go to Heaven? I am surprised by the number of people who don't think you can know that. Even more amazing is how many lost people have said they know for sure that if they died today, they would go to Hell. If they can know that, why can't we know whether we would be going to Heaven when we die? Look at what the Bible says:

- Verily, verily, I say unto you, He that believeth on me hath everlasting life (John 6:47).

- ...if thou shalt confess with thy mouth the Lord Jesus, and shalt believe in thine heart that God hath raised him from the dead, thou shalt be saved (Romans 10:9).

Not that you *might* be saved, but you *shall* be saved!

- For whosoever shall call upon the name of the Lord *shall* be saved (Romans 10:13).

- He that hath the Son hath life; and he that hath not the Son of God hath not life. These things have I written unto you that believe on the name of the Son of God; that ye may know that ye have eternal life, and that ye may believe on the name of the Son of God (I John 5:12-13).

We can *know* where we will spend eternity. That is very important in witnessing. If we know that when we die we'll go to Heaven, does it matter what a lost person says or does to us as we share our faith? No, it doesn't. Don't ever forget that as you boldly make your stand for Jesus.

Paul wrote in Philippians 1:21, "To me, to live is Christ, and to die is gain." Paul knew that this life was to be lived to please Jesus, and that when he died and went to Heaven it would be much better than living on earth. That is why Paul could walk into any town and have the craziest of events happen, but it just didn't matter to him. He knew that when he took his last breath, he would be in the arms of Jesus for all eternity. Do you have that same assurance? When you do, life is a whole lot of fun! Stay close to Jesus so He will be able to use you right up to your very last breath on earth!

If you were to die tonight and stand in front of God, and He asked, "Why should I let you into Heaven?" what would you tell Him?

This is a great follow-up to use with the previous question. Since it doesn't have a "yes" or "no" answer, it will draw more information from the person so you can know how to direct the conversation. This is also a great question because we all know that we will have to answer it one day. When all is said and done, we know we'll have to give an account of our lives. Did fifteen people at Columbine High School have to answer this question? Yes, they did. Two other people weren't thinking about it much or they wouldn't have done what they did.

Did Frank Sinatra, the great singer, have to answer this question? You bet he did. His theme song was "I Did It My Way." Frank Sinatra found out very quickly that doing it your way doesn't cut it when you stand in front of God.

Paul knew that when he took his last breath, he would be in the arms of Jesus for all eternity. Do you have that same assurance?

Are you doing it God's way? It is the only way to live this life—wholly pleasing to the God of this universe.

People typically answer this question by saying they are good enough to go to Heaven. But the Bible says, "For by grace are ye saved through faith; and that not of yourselves: it is the gift of God, not of works, lest any man should boast" (Ephesians 2:8-9). God has given us salvation as a free gift, and we must choose whether to accept it. If we got to Heaven by what *we* did and not by what Jesus did for us, we would brag about ourselves instead of bragging about that Guy with the nail-pierced hands and feet.

Isaiah 64:6 says, "But we are all as an unclean thing, and all our righteousnesses are as filthy rags." Think of that—to an all-holy and pure God, our righteous acts are just like filthy rags. And if our righteous acts are filthy, how bad does that make our sins? They are nasty and putrid before our holy, pure, and righteous God. As you can see, our good works will not get us into the kingdom of Almighty God.

> *If, to an all-holy and pure God, our righteous acts are like filthy rags, how bad does that make our sins?*

One day I heard a knock on my apartment door rather early in the morning. Normally that is not a good sign. My upstairs neighbor asked, "Have you been to your car yet?" This is not something you want to hear early in the morning! When I walked out to my car, I saw that someone must have really wanted my ten-disk CD player the night before—the thief shattered my window and stole it! In it at the time was the Bible on CD. All I hoped for was that, when the thief turned it on, he would hear something like, "Thou shalt not steal." That thought brought a big smile to my face!

I called the police to report the incident. It was raining when the policeman arrived, so we stood underneath my big golf umbrella. Because it started to rain hard and he was definitely a captive audience, I began to witness to him. When I asked him what he would tell God if he died tonight, and had to give a reason why he should be let into Heaven, he told me he was a very good guy, so he would be okay on Judgment Day.

Say What?

So I said, "Let me give you something to think about. Let's say your grandmother visits you on your birthday and gives you a brand new pair of Nike Air Jordan tennis shoes worth $120. You're very excited. Then you reach into your wallet and pull out $120 and give it to your grandmother. How would your grandmother feel?"

He replied, "Very insulted."

"Exactly," I continued. "She is trying to give you a gift, and you're trying to pay for it. The only thing you can do with a gift is accept it. That is exactly what God is trying to do for you. He is trying to give you the gift of the blood of Jesus shed on the cross for your sins, and you are trying to pay for it. You can't do that; you can only accept it as a gift."

The policeman nodded and said, "That is the best example I've ever heard." This Nike shoe example really makes sense to people. Give it a try.

A friend of mine uses this example when people say they are good enough to go to Heaven: If you take a burnt cake and put white icing on it, how does it look? Sure, it *looks* good—but when you take a bite out of it, how does it taste? Probably most of us have taken a bite out of a burnt cookie or piece of cake before, and were happy at first until we hit the burnt part. It tastes horrible. Well, it's the same with good works: We try to look good on the outside, but on the inside we are nasty and horrible—dead in our sins. We can't merely cover our sin; it must be gotten rid of. Something must change us from the inside out!

In Chapter 8, I will show you an excellent response to use when people say they are good enough to go to Heaven. It is straight out of the book of Romans, and will literally change the way you share your faith.

By the way, is there a right answer on Judgment Day? There certainly is. "I'm cleansed by the Blood!" First John

1:7 says that "if we walk in the light, as He is in the light, we have fellowship one with another, and the blood of Jesus Christ his Son cleanseth us from all sin." When you study different religions, you quickly realize that there is only one thing that will get rid of our sins—the pure cleansing blood of Jesus.

How do you get it? I John 1:9 says, "If we confess our sins, He is faithful and just to forgive us our sins, and to cleanse us from all unrighteousness." If His blood has cleansed you of all your sin, make sure you thank Him for that today!

When you die, what do you think is on the other side? What do you think is out there when you walk out of here?
This is probably my favorite question to use as part of a survey or in a conversation. I like it because it is very open-ended. It doesn't assume anything. Also, many people I talk with say they really love this question. It is amazing how many people love the question, yet have no clue what the right answer is! But that is where we come in and can let them know the correct answer.

When you ask this question, you will hear all kinds of answers—Heaven and Hell, Heaven and no Hell, nothing, reincarnation, unsure, an energy source that is out there, white light, etc. Some college students lately have even been answering, "Aliens." (I am not sure what they are being taught at these colleges, but it doesn't sound good!) To learn more about what people believe, talk with them awhile about their spiritual beliefs. Let God show you when to make the transition to talk about the eternal truth of the Bible and Jesus.

At Emory University in Atlanta, I used the survey approach to start a conversation with a student, then asked her this question. She told me that she believed in reincarnation.

I then asked, "Where do you get your information on reincarnation?" That opened up a thirty-minute conversation on what she believed. She was into a strange form of Buddhism, and had actually flown to France to study under a Buddhist teacher.

After I saw the opportunity to transition to the truth, we talked for another thirty minutes about the truth of the Bible, Jesus, sin, etc. At the end of our conversation, I gave her a tract and a book. (When people are really searching for the truth, I like to give them *God Doesn't Believe in Atheists,* by Ray Comfort, *The Case for Christ,* by Lee Strobel, or *More Than a Carpenter,* by Josh McDowell.)

She told me, "I would like to thank you for something. My beliefs are kind of strange; my friends have told me that. But you made me feel so comfortable talking about them that I really want to thank you."

She was right—her beliefs were pretty strange! But we need to let people feel comfortable talking about what they believe. Then when we transition to the Gospel they will listen to us.

Because I took time to build a rapport with her, she heard me when I talked about eternal truth. Being a listener also helps you learn about other people's beliefs, so you will see where to counter the lies Satan has fed them.

Why do you wear that cross?
An easy way to start a conversation with people is to ask about something they are wearing: T-shirt, jewelry, tattoo, etc. You can also use anything in your surroundings—a picture on a wall, nature, something that just happened, etc.—to steer a conversation in the eternal direction. When you ask people why they wear a cross, the most frequent answer is that it looks good. That is nowhere near the right answer.

So I usually ask, "Did you know that someone died on that cross?" The answer is often "no."

I then add, "Did you know that the cross is an instrument of death?" Again, people often say "no." Sometimes I ask, "Would you wear an electric chair around your neck?" That really makes people think. The cross is the electric chair of 2,000 years ago. Satan has reduced the most important and beautiful act in the history of the world into a mere piece of jewelry. I don't think our Savior was nailed to the cross thinking, *Won't this cross make a nice piece of jewelry in the future?*

This type of question works really well to get a conversation going. I have seen people commit their lives to Jesus after a conversation that started with their cross necklace.

I was in a yogurt shop one day and noticed that the young man behind the counter had "#1" on his necklace. I asked, "Darius, by the way, who is number 1?"

"I am," he boasted. "Why do you think I am wearing this necklace?" He seemed pretty excited about the idea. He was fifteen and thought the whole world revolved around him.

So I prompted him, "Darius, who do you think will be number one on the day you die?" He didn't have an answer, but he sure did before I left.

Another time, I was in a mall and noticed a guy wearing a long, black trench coat and a necklace with a real skull on it. I walked up to him and inquired, pointing to his necklace, "What in the world is that?" He told me that it was the skull of a muskrat—and he was walking around in public with this on!

He was a philosophy and religion major at Georgia State University. He definitely did not know the right answer to eternity, and I was able to talk with him about it for thirty minutes by using his necklace as a conversation starter.

Say What?

A friend of mine once got me a plane ticket for a 7:00 a.m. flight. (Would a real friend do something like that?) I arrived at the airport very early and was just trying to stay awake when I saw a college-age guy sit down about twenty seats away. He had a rainbow ribbon on his shirt and another one tied around his backpack. The rainbow ribbon is a symbol of the homosexual movement. So I put my head in my hands and thought, *God, it is way too early to witness!* I am not a big fan of early mornings! I knew I needed to chat with this guy, so I walked over and sat down next to him.

We can ask loaded questions. Our answers are loaded; why can't our questions be?

"Cute ribbon," I commented. "What does it stand for?"

Someone asked me once, "Isn't that a loaded question?" Of course, it is. We can ask loaded questions. Our answers are loaded; why can't our questions be?

The student told me that it stood for diversity. I asked him why he wore it and he answered, "We had a diversity week on our Catholic college campus, and I just think people need to let others believe what they want to believe, and stop telling them what they ought to believe."

I said, "Can I ask you a personal question? Are you a homosexual?" He said he wasn't, so I asked, "Why do you wear that ribbon then?" He repeated that we just need to let people believe what they want to believe.

That gave me a perfect opening to talk with him about absolute versus relative truth (which we'll cover in Chapter 10). Twenty minutes later when the airline gave the last call for his flight, he said, "Thank you so much for this conversation on absolute versus relative truth," and he took a tract booklet before boarding his plane. It was another great opportunity to share God's truth, based on something the person was wearing.

While I was in Miami, a high-school buddy and I stopped at a Starbucks. The college-age girl behind the counter had a couple of tattoos on her neck, so I asked her what they stood for. She explained that they were Egyptian symbols—one stood for earth and one stood for eternity.

That started a good, ten-minute conversation. She said she was really searching at that point in her life, so I gave her ten dollars to get a book that I wanted her to read. I encouraged her, shook her hand, and turned to leave.

When my friend and I got outside, he asked, "Mark, did you see her eyes when you turned around and left?"

"Bruce, I turned around and left; of course I didn't see her eyes!"

He said, "Her eyes got huge!"

She probably couldn't believe that a customer would take the time to witness to her, but especially that someone would give her ten dollars to buy a book. She could take that money and do anything she wanted with it. But it is important to put our money where our mouth is when it comes to belief.

Do you want to go to Heaven?
This is a great question because everyone answers, "Yes," or, "If there is one." Then you can follow up with, "Do you know how to get there?" or, "Can I show you how to get there?" Within a couple of questions you can be sharing the Gospel.

I was talking with a man from Norway and asked, "Do you want to go to Heaven?"

He responded, "Of course, I do."

I asked, "Do you know how to get there?"

"I have no clue!" he replied.

"Do you know how to get home to Norway from here?"

"Yes. I get in my car and drive to the airport. I get on a

plane and fly to Norway. Then I get in my car and go home."

So I said, "You know how to get to Norway, but you don't know how to get to Heaven?"

"Nope."

"Well, this is your lucky day," I said, "because I know how to get there!"

I don't actually believe in luck; I believe in the providential hand of an Almighty God. But is it possible that today could be a "lucky" day for someone who is planning to go to the mall or to work, but the God of this universe will send you across his path to bring the eternal information he so desperately needs?

Step out in faith, tell someone about the only way to Heaven—Jesus—and you just might be an answer to prayer!

What is the most important thing in the world to you? On the day you die, what do you think will be the mostt important thing to you?

This is another great survey question. It lets you know immediately what people value in life. To the first question you will often get answers like money, family, health, etc. Surprisingly, many times people will give the same answer on the second question as they did on the first.

While at an airport, I sat next to a gentleman and asked if he would help me on a project. He very nicely agreed. I asked, "What is the most important thing in the world to you?"

He gave a very common answer: "My family."

I continued, "On the day you die, what do you think will be the most important thing?"

He answered again, "My family." I asked what he meant and he explained, "I hope I have left behind enough money to take care of my family now that I am gone."

I asked, "Shouldn't the most important thing on that day be where you are going, and making sure that your family comes with you?"

"I've never thought about that before," he replied. We got into a great conversation, because these questions started him thinking about eternal matters.

Use Word Pictures

When you're talking to the lost, using word pictures can help the spiritual concepts to make more sense. After I have talked with someone about sin, repentance, and the blood of Jesus, I often use a word picture such as this: "It's as if you had a security tag on your jeans, and you walked out of a store. What would happen?"

When the person answers that the alarm would go off, I say, "Exactly. Picture Heaven the same way. At the gates of Heaven, imagine that there are sensors when you try to go in. What is the only thing that will set off the alarm as you try to enter?"

The usual response is, "My sin."

"That's right. Once you leave earth, your sin will set off the alarm. But if you have been cleansed of all your sin by the blood of Jesus Christ, can you walk through those gates?"

Step out in faith, tell someone about Jesus—the only way to Heaven—and you just might be an answer to prayer!

And the person always says "yes"—usually with a big smile! Most individuals have heard an alarm go off at a department store, and no one wants to be the culprit who sets it off.

Of course, none of us would want that to happen to us in an eternal sense. People can easily understand this example.

While I was witnessing to a youth at a mall, it seemed like the cross wasn't making much sense to him. I noticed a sign on a store window advertising a sale inside. I asked, "If your favorite store had a 50-percent-off sale on all clothing today, would you buy anything?"

He replied, "Of course I would."

"If they had a 99-percent-off sale on all clothing, would you buy anything?"

"Not only would I buy stuff, I would get something for my friends!" (I guess so, since the clothes would be about 50 cents per item!)

"If you would accept an offer of 99-percent off the price of some piece of clothing," I said, "why in the world wouldn't you accept the offer of 100-percent off of all your sin—past, present, and future—washed clean by the blood of Jesus Christ?" I could see he finally understood.

It is literally the best deal in the entire universe! Present it to people that way. Everyone loves a good deal. Jesus is the best thing that has ever happened in the history of this universe. Make sure people know that!

The next chapter looks at the biblical way to present the Gospel so it makes sense to the lost. Read it prayerfully and let it change the way you share your faith.

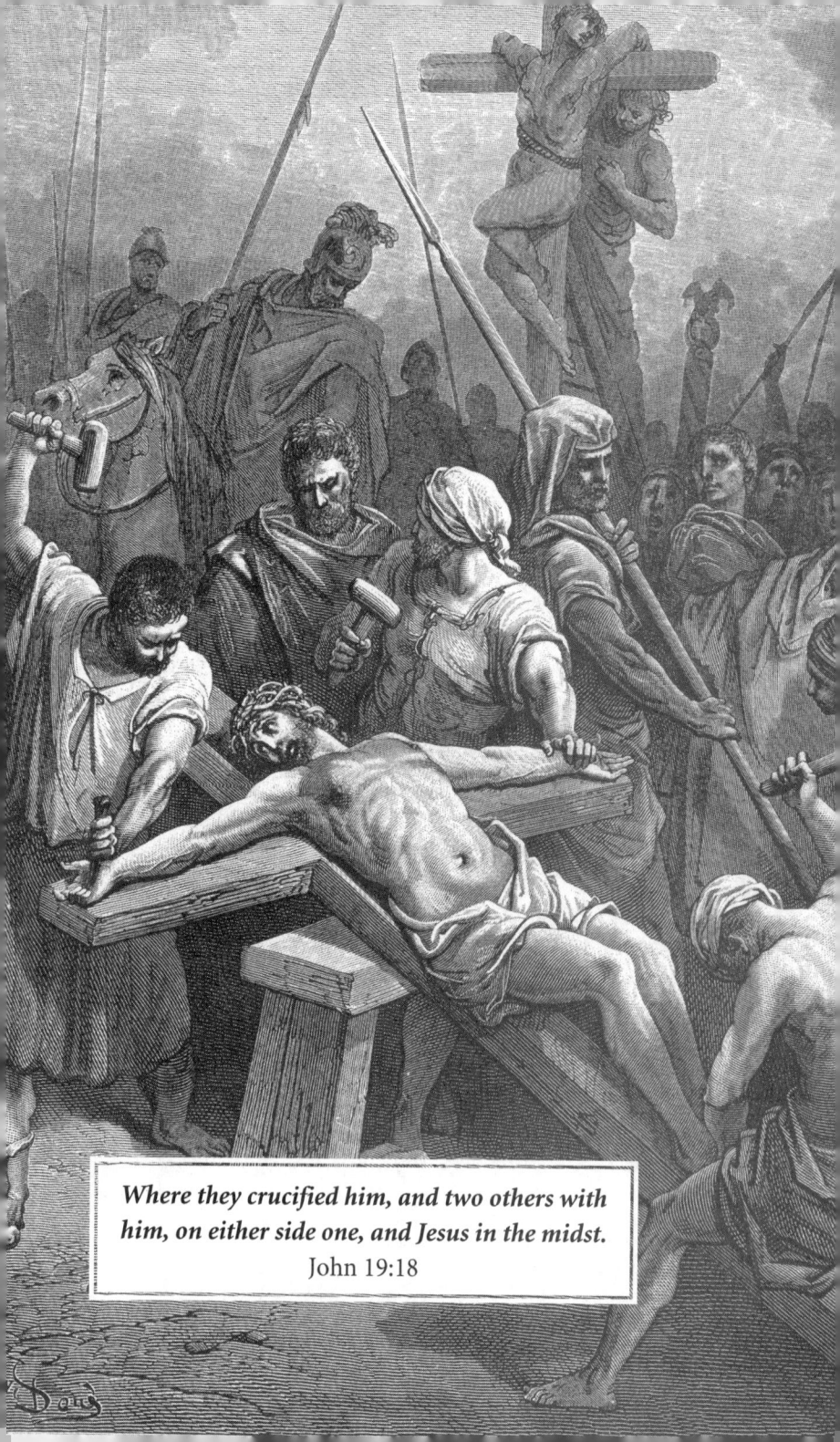

> *Where they crucified him, and two others with him, on either side one, and Jesus in the midst.*
> John 19:18

Chapter 8

Guilty!

"God be thanked when the Law so works as to take off the sinner from all confidence in himself! To make the leper confess that he is incurable is going a great way toward compelling him to go to that divine Savior, who alone is able to heal him. This is the whole end of the Law toward men whom God will save."
Charles Haddon Spurgeon

I cannot express how important this chapter is when sharing your faith. The information in this chapter is crucial for helping the lost understand their need for the Savior.

As you share your faith, there are three things you should talk about in every conversation. They are sin, repentance, and the cross. If you don't explain sin, people won't realize their need for a Savior. If you just share Jesus without discussing sin, then He becomes simply another religious figure like Mohammed or Buddha—people will not know why Jesus is the only answer or why they need Him.

When mentioning sin, most believers cite Romans 3:23, which says, "For all have sinned, and come short of the glory of God." For the lost to understand this verse, they need a definition for one of those words. They need to know what "sin" is. The Greek word for sin is an archery term and means "missing the mark"—there is a certain standard, and you have missed it. Imagine the bull's-eye on a target. If you shot an arrow at the target and missed the bull's-eye, you missed the mark: Sin!

ONE THING YOU CAN'T DO IN HEAVEN

To keep things simple, the lost need to know what the mark is so they would know whether they have made it or missed it. A very good approach when trying to understand biblical concepts is to let the Bible interpret the Bible. The answer is likely in the Bible somewhere, and not just in someone's opinion. That is why we must know the Word of Almighty God above all else. In this case, all we have to do is look a few verses earlier, and the answer is right there.

Romans 3:19-20 says, "Now we know that what things soever the Law saith, it saith to them who are under the Law: that every mouth may be stopped, and all the world may become guilty before God. Therefore by the deeds of the Law there shall no flesh be justified in His sight: for by the Law is the knowledge of sin."

The Law must be very important: it will not only stop people's mouths (keep them from attempting to justify themselves), but will show them that they are guilty before God. And it is the law that brings the knowledge of sin. So to understand what sin is, we need to know what this law is.

Psalm 19:7 informs us, "The Law of the Lord is perfect, converting the soul." This Law is perfect and converts the soul. What is this Law?

First John 3:4 says, "Whosoever committeth sin transgresseth also the Law: for sin is the transgression of the Law." Breaking the Law is sin, period.

The final clue in our search is in Romans 7:7, which says, "What shall we say then? Is the Law sin? God forbid! Nay, I had not known sin, but by the Law: for I had not known lust, except the Law had said, 'Thou shalt not covet.'"

If the Law says, "Thou shalt not covet," what exactly is the Law? "Thou shalt not covet" is the tenth of the Ten Commandments. So the Law must be referring to the Ten Commandments. Therefore, to know what sin is, we must know what the Ten Commandments are.

The Ten Commandments

The Ten Commandments can be found in both Exodus 20 and Deuteronomy 5, so they must be very important if they are stated twice by God in His holy Scriptures. Let's take a look at those Ten Commandments (from Exodus 20:3-10):

1. "Thou shalt have no other gods before me" (verse 3).

   This means God should be the focal point of your affections. The rich young ruler's god was money. What has your affection? Upon what do you meditate? When you lay your head on your pillow, what do you think about?

2. "Thou shalt not make unto thee any graven image, or any likeness of any thing that is in Heaven above, or that is in the earth beneath, or that is in the water under the earth; Thou shalt not bow down thyself to them, nor serve them: for I the Lord thy God am a jealous God, visiting the iniquity of the fathers upon the children unto the third and fourth generation of them that hate me; And showing mercy unto thousands of them that love me, and keep my commandments" (verses 4-6).

   The golden calf is probably the classic example of this from the Bible, although an idol doesn't have to be a tangible item. People also make an idol anytime they create a god that fits their own image. For example, I recently talked with a girl who claimed she was a Christian, but said that the god she believed in would not have created a Hell. That is not the God of the Bible; her god does not exist. Some people want a lawless god. That god also doesn't exist.

3. "You shall not take the name of the Lord your God in vain, for the Lord will not hold him guiltless who takes His name in vain" (verse 7).

Isn't it amazing how Satan has turned the most holy name in the universe into a name that we use flippantly or even as a curse word?

4. "Remember the Sabbath day, to keep it holy" (verse 8).

   No matter what you consider as keeping the Sabbath, you have broken it—and so has everyone else.

5. "Honour thy father and thy mother: that thy days may be long upon the land which the Lord thy God giveth thee. " (verse 12).

   This is an unconditional statement. It doesn't mean to honor your parents only if they give you the curfew you want, or if you think they are worthy, or anything else.

   Parents must be respected just because they are parents. This commandment has nothing to do with the worthiness of the parents, but only with the obedience of the children.

6. "Thou shalt not murder" (verse 13).

   The Hebrew says "murder," not "kill." God made this one very straightforward and simple. We might refer to abortion as a "choice," but it is still murder. It is the taking of innocent life. Jesus stated in the Sermon on the Mount that even hating or being angry with someone is the same as murder (Matthew 5:21-22). He judges the inside (our hearts) as well as the outside (our actions).

7. " Thou shalt not commit adultery" (verse 14).

   In the Sermon on the Mount, Jesus let us know that even looking with lust is the same as committing adultery (Matthew 5:27-28). Intent matters to God even if it may not matter to us.

8. "Thou shalt not steal" (verse 15).

   Theft is theft irrespective of value. Whether it is something small or large that is stolen, it is stealing in God's eyes. Stealing an answer from someone else's test and stealing time from an employer are also theft.

9. "Thou shalt not bear false witness against thy neighbour" (verse 16).

   Lying is wrong according to the God who says, "You shall know the truth, and the truth shall make you free" (John 8:32). Big lies, small lies, or white lies—all are lies to God.

10. "Thou shalt not covet thy neighbour's house, thou shalt not covet thy neighbour's wife, nor his manservant, nor his maidservant, nor his ox, nor his ass, nor any thing that is thy neighbour's" (verse 17).

    We covet before we steal. We covet before we commit adultery. Coveting opens up the floodgates of sin.

After reviewing the Ten Commandments, we may think we're not too bad if we have broken only a few of them. We may have missed the mark, but we think we can try again a little harder. However, the Bible says, "For whosoever shall keep the whole Law, and yet offend in one point, he is guilty of all" (James 2:10). If we have broken even one of the Ten Commandments, it is as if we have broken all of them. That is a pretty tough standard to follow. By that standard, Adolph Hitler, Jack the Ripper, Osama bin Laden, Billy Graham, Mother Teresa,

> *After reviewing the Ten Commandments, we may think we're not too bad if we have only broken a few of them.*

you, and I would all be equally guilty. That would put all of us in an eternal world of hurt, unless God provided a way to remove those sins that we have committed.

Numbers 32:23 warns us, "behold, ye have sinned against the Lord: and be sure your sin will find you out." We may try to hide our sin with good works every now and then, but our sin will surely find us out when we stand before the throne of Almighty God one day.

With this dismal reality, is there any way out, or are we just doomed by this Law? You'd better believe there is hope! And that hope is in the Son of God and in His blood.

Our Tutor

Galatians 3:24 explains that "the Law was our schoolmaster to bring us unto Christ, that we might be justified by faith." That's its purpose: The Law carries us right to Jesus. People attempt to be justified by their works, but the Law leads us to Jesus so that we can be justified by our faith, not by our works.

Greek is a very descriptive language. The Greek word for "schoolmaster" in Galatians 3:24 is also translated "tutor" or "teacher." It describes someone who walked or carried a child to school to make sure he arrived. Now do you see how the Law works? It will literally carry someone right to the cross, which is where we want to go in any witnessing conversation.

As I was listening to a sermon by a pastor who used to work in advertising, one statement in particular caught my attention.

In commercials, he explained, advertisers never say why their product is better than the competition. Instead, they create a desire for their product so people will want to buy it. Why, in commercials, do they place an attractive woman next to the car? They are trying to create a desire in you so that you will buy their product.

It occurred to me that that is exactly what the Law of God, the Ten Commandments, does for a sinner. Helping sinners see their personal guilt before a holy, just God will create in them a desire for whatever can get rid of their sin. They will now have a desire for Jesus and His cleansing blood.

Romans 2:15 says, "[They] show the work of the Law written in their hearts, their conscience also bearing witness, and their thoughts the meanwhile accusing or else excusing one another."

Here God clearly states that He has written His Law onto the hearts of mankind; their conscience will bear witness to this. *Conscience* (con+science) means "with knowledge." The lost will have knowledge of their sin.

By going through the Ten Commandments as we witness, we can help bring it to the forefront, and then they will see their need for the cross.

I was at a chapel service at a Christian college, waiting to speak, when they played a video of a missionary from the college working in Papua New Guinea. He stated that the people in that area had no written language; everything was passed down by word of mouth. Interestingly, they had a code of conduct to live by. One of their rules was to not touch their neighbor's wife.

This sounds like the seventh commandment to not commit adultery. Another rule was to not take other people's things. That is what the eighth commandment says when it tells us not to steal. Other rules were to not murder people or tell falsehoods about them. They didn't have writing, but the Law of God was written on their hearts, and they knew right from wrong.

Putting It into Practice

How do we use this way of talking about sin in a conversation? Actually, it is very simple. One Sunday morning while I was speaking at a church in Hilton Head, South Carolina, I gave everyone the assignment to share their faith with someone before returning to church that night. When I give an assignment, I like to do it myself. As I was driving back to the house where I was staying, I noticed a young man on a skateboard. I love talking to skateboarders—they are rarely Christian and are normally very open to conversation. I always begin by asking them to show me their best skateboard trick. They love showing off, and it helps to build friendship before starting a conversation.

This young man was an eighteen-year-old high-school senior. After we talked for a few minutes, I said, "Can I ask you an interesting question?"

"Sure," he replied.

I asked, "If you died tonight, are you 100-percent assured that you would go to Heaven?"

He quickly answered, "Yes."

"How do you know that to be true?"

"Because I am a really good guy."

"God gave us a standard to determine whether we are good," I explained, "and it's called the Ten Commandments. Have you heard of them?"

He replied that he had, so I said, "Well, let's see how you would do. Have you ever told a lie?"

"Yes."

"So what would that make you?" I asked.

"A liar."

"That's right. Have you ever stolen anything?"

"Yes, I have."

"What would that make you?"

"A thief," he responded.

"Have you ever lusted in your heart for someone?"

He replied, "Of course."

"Jesus said that is the same as committing adultery. Now, by your own admission, you have told me that you are a liar, a thief, and an adulterer at heart. You are not sounding half as good as you claimed to be just a few minutes ago."

Suddenly his head dropped. When the truth came out, he wasn't all that good by God's standard. No one is. So when I transitioned to the cross, it suddenly made sense to him.

One of the biggest lies Satan tells the lost is that they will be good enough for God on Judgment Day. If they helped an old lady across the road, threw a few dollars into the collection plate, had the best-kept yard in the neighborhood, etc., then they will be just fine on Judgment Day. Do you see how the Law works to break right through that lie?

> *One of the biggest lies Satan tells the lost is that they will be good enough for God on Judgment Day.*

I recently caught part of the movie *Saving Private Ryan*. At the end of the movie, Private Ryan, who had survived the battles of World War II, was now an older gentleman. To assure himself that he was fulfilling a commitment he had made to a dying soldier, he appealed to his wife, "Tell me I've led a good life. Tell me I'm a good person." He was trying to justify his life by being a good man. But the problem was that he was asking his wife. Another person will not judge whether we are good enough.

The Bible explicitly states that when we die, we will stand in front of God—not anyone else (Romans 2:16; 2 Corinthians 5:10; Revelation 20:11–15). It is only His opinion that matters, and by His standard we are all in a lot of trouble and in desperate need of a Savior. Isn't it nice to know that God has provided one, and He is available to all who truly want Him?

A Game Show

One day I was flying back to Atlanta from Colorado, where I had spoken at a camp hosted by Summit Ministries. (It is the top Christian leadership camp in the country. If you want to learn how to defend the Christian worldview and how to make a bold stand for Christ wherever you are, contact Summit Ministries at www.summit.org or 719-685-9103.)

A woman was sitting two seats over, with some of her belongings in the empty seat between us. I glanced over and noticed a DMB sticker with a lot of autographs. DMB stands for the Dave Matthews Band, a secular band that is popular with teens and college-age folks.

I asked her what the sticker was for, and she explained that she had been to the Dave Matthews concert the night before in Denver. She said there were 70,000 people there. That is a lot of people! Be praying for the day when we will see 70,000 coming to stadiums for church services, and not just when Billy Graham comes to town.

When I asked how she got the band members' autographs, she answered, "I am a disc jockey from a rock station in Baltimore, and I was allowed to go backstage." That was pretty cool, and it was obvious she was proud of that. After we chatted for a while, I said, "Can I ask you an interesting question?" She replied, "Sure."

"When you die, what do you think is on the other side?"

"I love that question," she answered. "I grew up Lutheran, so I think there is a Heaven and a Hell, but I have been searching out reincarnation lately." So we talked a little about reincarnation. Eventually I said, "The Bible, being true, lets us know that there is a Heaven and a Hell. That being the case, if you died today, which place would you go to?"

She said, "Oh, I would definitely be going to Heaven."

"How do you know that to be true?"

With an air of confidence she replied, "Because I am a good person."

I am amazed that there is as much evil in the world as there is, because everyone I meet is such a good person! I responded, "God has given us a standard of good and bad, and it's called the Ten Commandments. Let's see how you are doing."

She eagerly agreed. It was as if this were a game show, and she wanted to see how she would do on the questions!

I began, "Have you ever told a lie?"

"Yes."

"So what does that make you?"

Rather arrogantly she replied, "A sinner," almost like she was proud of it.

I said, "No—more specifically, what does that make you?"

Suddenly she dropped her head; she didn't want to look at me. You see, the Law of God is written on our hearts. With her head lowered she said, "I don't want to say."

I assured her, "It's okay to say, because I've done that too."

"A liar," she answered.

I continued, "Have you ever stolen anything?"

With her head back up, she said "yes." Again, I prompted her, "What does that make you?"

"A thief."

"Have you ever lusted in your heart for someone?"

She responded, "Yes."

"Jesus says that is the same as committing adultery. Have you ever taken the name of the Lord in vain?"

"Yes."

"That's called blasphemy. Have you ever been angry at someone?"

She said, "Most definitely." That's an interesting answer.

"Jesus says that is the same as committing murder," I explained. "Now, by your own admission, you have told me that you are a liar, a thief, an adulterer, a blasphemer, and a murderer. Would you be guilty or not guilty on Judgment Day?"

Note that I never told her that she was a sinner. She told me that she was all of those things. That is why you never have to worry about offending people when you use the Ten Commandments in witnessing. The lost are just verbally admitting what they already know in their hearts.

"I would be guilty," she answered.

"Would that mean you would go to Heaven or Hell?"

She said, "Hell." Notice that she went from being a good person to telling me that she was going to Hell, in all of about five minutes!

I continued, "If you could go from guilty to not guilty on Judgment Day, would that be good news?" By this time, when people realize their sin, they can't wait to hear the good news.

She said, "Yes!"

I then took the time to share with her about repentance, the cross, and what the blood of Jesus could do for her. She was very interested when I shared the cross with her because she now knew her need for it. This isn't "Jeopardy"! Often when we share our faith, we want to give people the answer (Jesus)—and they don't know what the question is yet! Make sure that you share Jesus only *after* people recognize their need for Him. His shed blood then makes sense to them. If I walked around saying, "Four, four, four," you would think I was crazy. But if I first asked, "What does two plus two equal?" then stating "four" makes sense. Identify the problem first, and then give the answer.

GUILTY!

At the end of the flight, she asked me for my mail and e-mail addresses to keep in touch. When we got off the plane in Atlanta, she needed directions to her next flight, so I gave them to her. She then looked at me and asked, "Can I give you a hug?"

Here we were, total strangers at the start. I very lovingly shared the truth with her, making sure I talked about sin. She appreciated it so much that she felt comfortable enough to want a hug at the end of the conversation. Step out in faith and truly witness and act like Jesus, and God will show you more cool things than you could ever imagine!

It Really Works!

I like to witness in the bar sections of towns, especially in the summer. These areas are usually bustling with people hanging outside or walking from bar to bar, and many of them are eager to engage in a conversation. One Saturday night in Buckhead, the bar area of Atlanta, I used my survey approach to begin a conversation with a couple in their early twenties.

After the young woman gave me an answer, the guy said, "There is a Heaven and a Hell. And when I die I am going to Heaven because I keep the Ten Commandments." It didn't take long to get right to the point! "Okay," I began, "let's see how you are doing. Have you ever told a lie?"

He said, "Nope."

I was thinking, *We have all told a lie. You just lied to me in your answer!* So I responded, "What do you mean 'nope'?"

"I have only stretched the truth before."

He thought he had me, but I asked, "How far do you have to stretch the truth before it becomes a lie?" He smiled and admitted, "Okay, I have lied before."

"What does that make you?" I asked.

"A liar."

"Have you ever stolen something?"

"Yes."

"What does that make you?"

"A thief."

I continued, "Have you ever lusted in your heart for a girl before?"

His answer was, "No."

His girlfriend quickly pointed a finger at him and said, "You've lusted for *me* before!" He's in trouble now! When she said that, he responded with a curse word—it was the Lord's name in vain.

I said, "Wait a minute. There is another one you have broken! You are 0 for 4 and we have only gone through four of the Commandments! Would you be guilty or not guilty on Judgment Day?" He said "guilty," and you know where we went from there. Using the Ten Commandments really is incredibly effective.

After I spoke at a church in Kansas, people came forward at the end of the service to give testimonies. One woman said she had been going to church for twenty-six years, but that this was the first time she could say that she was cleansed of her sin and was right with Jesus Christ.

During the sermon, I'd spent time talking about witnessing and discussed how to use the Ten Commandments. She said that she knew about Jesus, but didn't fully understand why she needed Him. The Ten Commandments made her realize her guilt before God, and drove her right to the cross!

On another occasion, I was speaking at a Fellowship of Christian Athletes meeting at Clemson University. It is always a fun place to speak because they have a dynamic group with about eight hundred students at a meeting.

As I gave a talk on the Ten Commandments, I discussed what each Commandment was about, and explained that

Guilty!

each one of us has broken each one of them. I then illustrated how to use the Ten Commandments in witnessing. Afterwards, people came up to ask questions.

As I was talking with others, I noticed a young man walk up and stand a few feet away. The look on his face said he really wanted to talk with me.

As soon as I could, I walked over to him and asked if I could help him with anything. He blurted out, "I am not right with God."

I asked what he meant, and he replied, "I am in a fraternity here at Clemson. All I do is drink—that's it. Last week while I was at the fraternity house drinking, I was lying on the floor, and I looked up to God and said, 'God, I am not right with you. If I died today, I would die and go to Hell; and I don't want to go there.'" Now, just a few days later, he walked into this talk I was giving—the first Christian event he had ever been to!

People who are ready to repent of their sins and come to Jesus really don't need to repeat a prayer after you.

I asked him, "Do you want to get right with God?"

"Yes, I do."

"Have you ever told a lie before?"

His response was, "Yes, and I know I am not right with God!"

I was starting to walk him through the Ten Commandments, like I normally do, completely forgetting that I had just given a fifty-minute talk on them! He knew his guilt before God. So we talked about the purpose of the cross, and I asked if he wanted to walk away from this lifestyle, repent of his sins, and commit his life to Jesus.

"Yes, I do," he repeated.

When someone is ready to commit his life to Christ, let

him pray. People who are ready to repent of their sins and come to Jesus really don't need to repeat a prayer after you. God is already working on their hearts—and if He isn't, having them repeat words not only will not help, it will hurt! Just let them pray.

After praying, we talked about assurance of salvation. I asked if he had a Bible so he could get started reading. He didn't, so I called one of the FCA guys over to help him get a Bible and get plugged into a men's Bible study group.

I learned a few months later that this young man had already read the entire New Testament! It is very important to get people lost before you can get them saved.

When you use the Ten Commandments to help people see their sin before God, they grab hold of Jesus and don't let go! And that is how it should be.

Proving the Case
On a flight back from a speaking engagement in Minnesota, I sat next to a gentleman who was listening to music on his CD player. He had to turn it off as we taxied out, so I took the opportunity to begin a conversation.

I discovered he was a gay man who lived in Atlanta, but he had flown to Minnesota for the weekend to visit his partner, a professor at the University of Minnesota. I was excited about the chance to witness to him.

After we had talked awhile I said, "Can I ask you an interesting question?"

He said, "Sure."

"When you die," I asked, "what do you think is on the other side? What do you think is out there when we walk out of here?"

"That's a good question," he replied. "I'm not really sure, but I think that there is nothing."

Guilty!

"How do you know that to be true?" I asked. He didn't have any evidence to back up his position.

"Where do you get your information that there is nothing after we die?" He didn't have a book or anything else upon which to base his belief. You will find this to be very typical.

So then he asked me, "What do *you* believe?"

That is a great point in a conversation! But always remember, people are not interested just in what you believe, but in why you believe it. How did you arrive at that conclusion? What evidence did you use to make that decision? That's what they are looking for.

I explained my belief that there is a God and a Heaven and Hell, and that it was the evidence that was very interesting to me. I took time to discuss proofs for God as well as proofs that the Bible is true.

He remarked, "You ought to be a lawyer. You are arguing your case very, very well!" I wasn't actually arguing with him, but I was proving the case well—and he appreciated it. He used to be a lawyer, so he enjoyed someone using logic to make him think. Once I proved the Bible true, I told him that it says there is a Heaven and a Hell, so which place did he want to go to? Of course, he said "Heaven."

I asked, "Do you know what it takes to get there?"

"Probably being a good guy."

"God has given us a standard for being good," I said, "so let's see how you are doing. Have you ever told a lie?"

He answered, "Yes."

After taking a couple of minutes to review the Ten Commandments, I said, "Now that you have told me that you are a liar, thief, adulterer, blasphemer, and murderer, would you be guilty or not guilty on Judgment Day?" He admitted he would be guilty.

"Would that mean Heaven or Hell?"

"I guess that means Hell."

"If you could go from being guilty to not guilty on Judgment Day," I asked, "would that be good news?"

His eyes suddenly widened as he said, "I know exactly where you are going with this."

"Where am I going with this?"

He repeated with eyes still wide, "I know exactly where you are going with this!"

I asked again, "Where am I going with this?"

He said, "Does this have anything to do with the initials J. C.?"

I laughed a little and said, "Oh, do you have a hard time saying the name of Jesus?"

The man had grown up in a Baptist church, so in his heart he knew the truth of Galatians 3:24—that the Law leads us to Jesus. He now realized why he would need Jesus to get rid of all his sin. He knew about Jesus, but now he understood the reason He came to earth two thousand years ago.

At the end of the flight, he told me, "You have made the flight go by very quickly. Thank you for that, and thank you for the good conversation." He loves his sin too much right now, but a seed has been planted in his life. I am praying that I will see him in Heaven one day, or will see him another day down here to water that seed.

God's Word Will Not Return Void

When the door opened for me to speak at a retreat for a certain denomination, I went, even though that denomination has the reputation of being liberal in their interpretation of Scripture. I spoke to three hundred teenagers on Saturday, before the big event on Sunday. I gave a basic talk on the Ten Commandments and how to use them in witnessing.

Guilty!

I had barely made it through the Commandments when a man walked up to me from the side and asked me to have the teens stand up and stretch. (They were sitting on a hard floor.)

Then he added, "You have five minutes to finish." I glanced at my watch and saw that it was twenty-five minutes less than what they told me I had! Then it hit me—they were throwing me off the stage! It was amazing to see the Ten Commandments work on people's hearts.

I found out later that a female priest told a friend of mine, "You must talk with that guy. Tomorrow when he speaks he cannot mention homosexuality. There are kids who have brought their two lesbian mothers with them to this retreat."

What was interesting was that I had never mentioned homosexuality in my talk; I merely said that lusting in your heart is the same as committing adultery. But when we cite God's holy standard, the Holy Spirit can work on the conscience to convict people of their sin.

Needless to say, it was not the best weekend of my life. The talks didn't seem to go very well. But always remember that "we walk by faith, not by sight" (2 Corinthians 5:7). What we can see is not all that is happening in the spiritual realm. I received an e-mail a month later from a youth pastor who attended the retreat. There was a very tough teen whom he hadn't been able to reach in the two years he'd been in the youth group. He asked the teenager what he thought about the retreat. The teen replied, "It was a great experience. I'll remember it for the rest of my life." Then the youth pastor asked him, "What did you think of that Mark Cahill guy?" The young man's face lit up as he said, "If I remember anything about this retreat, it will be the talk that man gave. It was the best talk I've ever heard."

I was down in the dumps about that weekend, but God was at work in that teen's life and was able to reach him. Two weeks later, I got a letter from another teen who had been at the retreat. She said, "I have heard God speak to me twice in my life. Once was in 7th grade, and the other time was during your talk at that retreat."

Remember, do not always go by what you see. Keep walking by faith and trusting the Lord; be obedient to Him and no one else! If you're faithful to share God's Word, He promises that it will not return void.

The Most Pressing Need

Let's look at what some great men from the past, who boldly preached the Word of God, had to say about using the Law of God (the Ten Commandments) in witnessing.

And if it was important to the biblical writers and these great men of God to preach the Law, it is good enough for you and me.

> *Dr. J. Gresham Machen:* "A new and more powerful proclamation of [the] Law is perhaps the most pressing need of the hour; men would have little difficulty with the Gospel if they had only learned the lesson of the Law."

> *Charles Finney:* "It is of great importance that the sinner should be made to feel his guilt, and not have the impression that he is unfortunate. Do not be afraid, but show him the breadth of the divine Law, and the exceeding strictness of its precepts. Make him see how it condemns his thoughts and life. By a convicted sinner, I mean one who feels himself condemned by the Law of God as a guilty sinner. I remark that this [the Law] is the rule, and the only just rule by which the guilt of sin can be measured... Every man need only

consult his own conscience faithfully and he will see that it is equally affirmed by the mind's own intuition to be right."

D. L. Moody: "God, being a perfect God, had to give a perfect Law, and the Law was given not to save men, but to measure them. I want you to understand this clearly, because I believe hundreds and thousands stumble at this point. They try to save themselves by trying to keep the Law; but it was never meant for men to save themselves by.

"Ask Paul why [the Law] was given. Here is his answer, 'That every mouth may be stopped, and all the world may become guilty before God' (Romans 3:19). The Law stops every man's mouth. I can always tell a man who is near the kingdom of God; his mouth is stopped. This, then, is why God gives us the Law—to show us ourselves in our true colors."

John MacArthur: "Every unredeemed human being, Jew or Gentile, is under the Law of God and accountable to God. The final verdict, then, is that unredeemed mankind has no defense whatsoever and is guilty of all charges. The defense must rest, as it were, before it has opportunity to say anything, because the omniscient and all-wise God has infallibly demonstrated the impossibility of any grounds of acquittal. Absolute silence is the only possible response."

John Wesley: "The first use of [the Law], without question, is to convince the world of sin. By this is the sinner discovered to himself. All his fig-leaves are torn away, and he sees that he is 'wretched and poor and miserable, blind and naked.' The Law flashes conviction on every side. He feels himself a mere sinner. He has nothing to pay. His 'mouth is stopped' and he stands 'guilty before God.'

"The very first end of the Law [is], namely, convicting men of sin; awakening those who are still asleep on the brink of Hell… The ordinary method of God is to convict sinners by the Law, and that only. The Gospel is not the means which God hath ordained, or which our Lord Himself used, for this end."

> *"The ordinary method of God is to convict sinners by the Law, and that only."*

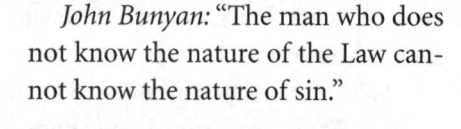

John Bunyan: "The man who does not know the nature of the Law cannot know the nature of sin."

Martyn Lloyd-Jones: "The trouble with people who are not seeking for a Savior, and for salvation, is that they do not understand the nature of sin. It is the peculiar function of the Law to bring such an understanding to a man's mind and conscience. That is why great evangelical preachers 300 years ago in the time of the Puritans, and 200 years ago in the time of Whitefield and others, always engaged in what they called preliminary 'Law work.'"

I am forever indebted to Ray Comfort of Living Waters Publications for opening my eyes to the proper use of the Ten Commandments. It was a missing piece to my witnessing that I really needed, and the Lord sent him to me at just the right time. Ray's audiotape *Hell's Best Kept Secret* and his book *Revival's Golden Key* are excellent resources. You can order them at www.livingwaters.com or at 800-437-1893.

Repent!

One topic that we must talk about when we discuss sin is repentance. It's a word that we don't use much in witnessing, and apparently a word that some people don't want to use at all. Yet "repent" and its various forms is used over one hundred times in the Bible. It must be a very important word then, and something that we must understand.

John the Baptist preached in the wilderness, "Repent ye: for the kingdom of Heaven is at hand" (Matthew 3:2).

Jesus preached this same message of repentance. Mark 1:14-15 records that Jesus came to Galilee saying, "The time is fulfilled, and the kingdom of God is at hand: repent ye, and believe the Gospel."

When Jesus sent out the twelve disciples two by two, "they went out, and preached that men should repent" (Mark 6:12). If Jesus sent the disciples out to preach that people must repent of their sins, we ought to be doing the same.

"Repent" consists of two Latin syllables: re+pent, which means "again+think" or "think again" or "to rethink."

The Complete Word Study New Testament, by Dr. Spiros Zodhiates, says the main word used for "repent" in the Greek is *metanoéo*. He says that word means "to repent with regret accompanied by a true change of heart toward God ... It signifies a change of mind consequent to retrospection, indicating regret for the course pursued and resulting in a wiser view of the past and future. Most importantly, it is distinguished from *metaméllomai*, [which means] to regret one's actions because of their consequences."

So you see, repentance is not feeling bad because we got caught doing something wrong. True repentance comes when we change our mind about our sin so our actions will not continue to be the same.

The difference is made clear by Paul in 2 Corinthians 7:10, "For godly sorrow worketh repentance to salvation not to be repented of: but the sorrow of the world worketh death."

One Thing You Can't Do in Heaven

I have a friend whose native tongue is Hebrew. He says that ancient and modern Hebrew are the same except for words that have been created for modern inventions like the telephone, the computer, and so on. So every day, school children in Israel visit the Dome of the Book museum in Jerusalem, where a 2800-year-old scroll of the book of Isaiah is on display—and the kids can just read it!

My friend told me, speaking of repentance, that the two Hebrew words for "repent"—*kha-zah-rah* and *tshu-vah*—both mean "to return." This tells us that we should, by the power of God, hate the things of the world so much, after seeing them through God's eyes, that we can turn our back on them and just walk away—returning to our Creator as our guide and source. Then, as a new creature, we head out into a new life of serving our Lord and Savior Jesus Christ!

When I witness to the lost, I talk about sin, repentance, and the cross. If people do not want to repent of their sins, do they really want to surrender their life to Jesus? I am in no way saying that someone can become a Christian and then the very next day be perfect and preaching like Billy Graham. But I am saying that, if there is no desire to turn away from sin, the person is *not* really making a true heart commitment to the Savior. In John 6:44, Jesus says, "No man can come to me, except the Father which hath sent me draw him…." If God is drawing someone *to* Him, He would also be drawing the person *away* from his sin.

If God is drawing someone to Him, He would also be drawing the person away from his sin.

I was sitting around talking one night with a young man I had met at a camp. He was telling me about his life and confessed that he had been using cocaine for the past thirty days. About forty-five minutes into the conversation he asked,

"Is this the point where you are going to start talking to me about Jesus?"

I said, "No."

He looked rather surprised. "You're not?"

I explained that he was not ready for Jesus and that it was not his day to get saved. He did not hate his sin enough to want to repent and walk away from it. He loved the world way too much. What was interesting was that he didn't argue with me one bit. He didn't want to get saved that day; he wanted to use drugs. He had gone to a Christian high school, so he knew all the right answers. But the issue was repentance, and he didn't want to do that.

> *"To make a so-called profession without a lifestyle change is a profession without the possession of eternal life."*

When you witness, remember to take time to talk with people and explain salvation. It is the most important decision they will ever make, so they really need to understand the decision they are making. It takes more than two minutes to buy a car or to select a college.

When I speak, I do not do two-minute altar calls. If I didn't give a salvation message, I don't do an altar call at all. If individuals want to come forward and talk to someone about salvation, they are free to do so. I explain that with Christianity one cannot drink beer, use drugs, have sex, cheat on tests, and disobey his parents, then get saved and continue to drink beer, use drugs, have sex, cheat on tests, and disobey his parents. I just can't find that in the Bible.

When a person is born again, his life changes. It certainly doesn't mean that we become perfect when we get saved; there is definitely a sanctification process, as we grow in our faith to become like Christ. But there must be a *desire* to change, or there won't be any change.

Ann Landry, an intercessor who prays for me, wrote this to me in an e-mail: "When we leave the cross out of our calling men to Jesus, we preach a Gospel that cannot cure men of sin. God constantly tells us that His people are separated, holy, distinctly different from the world.

"To make a so-called profession without a lifestyle change is a profession without the possession of eternal life. When Christ moves into a life, the life changes. The Holy Spirit is holy and moves men to holiness. Please, please call them to repent of their sins." The life of a sinner definitely changes when the Spirit of God moves into that life. My high school buddies look at my life now and say, "Cahill, you are different." It is a bit like those "before and after" weight-loss pictures, but in a spiritual way. They know the old Mark Cahill and can definitely see changes in the new one.

I was talking with two teenagers at a state fair. After chatting for a while, I went through the Ten Commandments with them, then moved on to the topic of repentance. The response of both was, "Yes, I want to walk away from this life. I hate this life that I am leading." You will be amazed at how many times you will hear that from people. These teens were drinking and using drugs, and at seventeen years of age they already knew that lifestyle was a dead-end street.

A Surrendered Life

Please remember that people don't become Christians by "asking Jesus into their heart" or by signing a decision card. Jesus said that we must be born again (John 3:3). John 3:16 also lets us know that we must believe in Jesus. But belief is much more than just an acknowledgment of the facts. It is to be persuaded or convinced, and to put your complete trust and confidence in something. It is more than just using the lips; it is using your heart also.

GUILTY!

Romans 10:9 says "that if thou shalt confess with thy mouth the Lord Jesus, and shalt believe in thine heart that God hath raised him from the dead, thou shalt be saved."

We are not confessing simply that we don't want to go to Hell and we want to go to Heaven; we are confessing that Jesus is Lord! God wants a total commitment of our whole being. I like to ask people if they want to surrender their life to Jesus, and by that I mean giving Him complete control of their life.

By the way, how do you think of Jesus? Do you believe in Him or do you trust in Him? Belief is trust with your mind; faith is trusting with your life. Jesus wants every bit of our entire being to serve Him, not just the part that we want to give Him. We can say we have a relationship with God, but He will know by the reality of what is seen in our lives.

Second Corinthians 5:17 says, "Therefore if any man be in Christ, he is a new creature: old things are passed away; behold, all things are become new." You are not a new and improved version of the old you, you are a new creature in God! God is not an additive in your life; He is a transformer and a redeemer of sinners. Jesus is not some ticket that will save people from Hell; He is the Savior of the world and wants us to submit to Him. He wants to completely change every area of our lives. When we repent of sin, commit our lives to Jesus, and make Him Lord, our lives will be different!

You are not a new and improved version of the old you, you are a new creation in God!

And please remember, that is a good thing! I wouldn't change my life now for anything. I have lived on both sides of the fence, both in total sin and in trying to live for God. I choose this life over that sinful lifestyle any day of the week.

Repenting means to make a turn, and that is what you see in the true Christian life.

A true Christian will have a hunger for the things of God —for witnessing, prayer, and Bible study. Are you faithfully sharing Jesus with the lost? Are you seeking God's face every day in prayer? Do you read the Word daily? Dwight Moody said, "The Bible will keep you from sin, but sin will keep you from the Bible."

Joshua 1:8 tells us how to have success in the Christian life: "This book of the Law shall not depart out of thy mouth; but thou shalt meditate therein day and night, that thou mayest observe to do according to all that is written therein: for then thou shalt make thy way prosperous, and then thou shalt have good success."

For success in witnessing, the questions in the next chapter will help you as you talk with others about the Lord.

And when they had crucified him, they parted his garments, casting lots upon them, what every man should take.

Mark 15:24

CHAPTER 9

FOUR DEADLY QUESTIONS

"If there existed only one man or woman who did not love the Savior, and if that person lived among the wilds of Siberia, and if it were necessary that all the millions of believers on the face of the earth should journey there, and every one of them plead with him to come to Jesus before he could be converted, it would be well worth all the zeal, labor, and expense. If we had to preach to thousands year after year, and never rescued but one soul, that one soul would be full reward for all our labor, for a soul is of countless price."
CHARLES HADDON SPURGEON

When witnessing to someone, it's very important to ask the person questions. Christians often make the mistake of rushing into their presentation of the Gospel when they haven't really talked with the person yet.

Finding out what people believe, and why they believe it, is essential in a good witnessing situation. Keep in mind that you don't have to do all of the proving in a conversation. Ask non-believers to try to prove their positions on eternity and God.

At the Summit Ministries Christian leadership camps where I speak, we teach students something called the "four deadly questions." These questions are fantastic. Although they are very simple, they're also very thought-provoking.

Four Deadly Questions

The questions are designed to help people realize that they cannot defend their positions. Then we can come behind and defend our position in love. Make sure that you don't use these questions as a weapon; they can make people look foolish, which will certainly not make them receptive to your message. They are intended only as aids to help you gain more information, not to inflict harm. At Summit we suggest that students use them with their professors in college classrooms. When these questions are asked in a gentle, loving way, they prove to be very effective in helping students make their point. So let's take a look at these "four deadly questions."

1. What do you mean by that?
With this question you can prompt people to define words they are using. The more information you have about an individual's views, the better you can direct the conversation.

Many times a person will tell me that he is a Christian. So I ask, "What do you mean by 'Christian'?" Numerous people answer the question by stating that they go to church. By the way, does going to church make you a Christian? Of course it doesn't. Does going to the garage make you a car? Does going into a McDonald's make you a hamburger? Going to church is something a Christian should do, but it doesn't make someone a Christian.

I was talking with a young man at Georgia Tech who told me that he was a Christian. I asked what he meant by "Christian," and he answered, "I am bought and saved by the blood of Jesus Christ!" I said, "Okay, easy, young man!" He certainly knows what he believes, as all of us should.

When someone tells me he is into the New Age movement, I ask, "What do you mean by 'New Age'?" The New Age can encompass all kinds of things, from reincarnation, to crystals, to Wicca, etc. So this question will help identify what the person means by that term.

If someone says he is agnostic, ask, "What do you mean by 'agnostic'?" Some people mean "atheist" but say "agnostic," and vice versa. (An atheist is someone who denies there is a God; an agnostic doesn't rule out the possibility of God but believes God's existence is unknowable.) Find out what the person believes it means: then you can direct the conversation accordingly.

2. How do you know that to be true?

When an individual is explaining his views, one of the most beneficial questions you can ask is how he knows that a statement he made is true. What evidence does he have to back up his position?

One person told me that there were eighteen authors of the Book of Matthew. I asked him, "How do you know that to be true?" Did he have any evidence to back up his position? Absolutely none. Of course, Matthew wrote the Book of Matthew, but some very liberal religion professors are teaching untruths about the authorship of the Bible.

When people say they are 100-percent assured that if they died today they would go to Heaven, ask, "How do you know that to be true?" You will get some interesting answers, from "Jesus" to "being a good person."

And if they mention being a good person, you know what to say from there—just go through the Ten Commandments.

One person I spoke with claimed that Jesus did not rise from the dead. I asked him how he knew that to be true. He didn't have a single bit of evidence to back up his statement. He wasn't aware of all the evidence I shared with him that conclusively proves Jesus *did* rise from the dead.

Four Deadly Questions

When the topic of evolution comes up, people will often comment on the age of the earth, which they believe to be billions of years. Ask them how they know. You will find that they have no actual evidence to back up that position. A friend of mine who travels the country to speak about creation versus evolution shows in his presentations that most dating methods reveal a very young earth. Evolutionists, however, just choose the dating method that supports their position, which is not good science. Asking this question helps people dig deeper for the truth.

I gave them the evidence showing that what they believed was not based in truth. In return, they gave me instant respect.

One day in a mall I noticed three college-age guys sitting at a table in the food court. When I walked over, pulled up a chair, and sat down with them, they looked at me like I was crazy. So I asked, "You've never had a total stranger sit down with you in the mall before?"

"No."

"Well, this is your first time."

They said, "Okay," and began to talk with me! During the conversation one of the guys asked, "You're a Christian, aren't you?"

"Yes, I am," I replied.

He asked, "You believe the Bible is true, don't you?"

"Yes, I do."

"You can't believe that book is true. There is no way that book is true!" he said. "It was written down by King James in 1611. It can't be true."

Notice that he said the Bible was *written* in 1611. Is that true? It's not even close to a true statement. King James had the Bible *translated* from Hebrew and Greek into the

King's English at that time. So the Bible was only *translated* then, but it was *written* from about 2000 BC to 100 AD. So I asked, "Are you sure you want to say that?" I then gave them the evidence showing that what they believed was not based on fact. In return, they gave me instant respect, and listened to everything else I said during the conversation.

3. Where do you get your information?

This question identifies the information source for what the person believes. Many times, you'll find that there isn't one. The person is basing his eternal future on something he hasn't fully investigated. One guy told me that he believed in reincarnation, so I asked, "Where do you get your information on reincarnation?"

He replied, "I believe in my heart that it's true."

"Have you ever believed something in your heart that turned out to be wrong?"

"Most definitely."

"Could you be wrong on reincarnation?"

"Oh, I could definitely be wrong!" he responded. Within thirty seconds, he went from believing in reincarnation to admitting he could be wrong!

When people say they are good enough to go to Heaven, ask them where they get their information. Many people claim that they find it in the Bible. When they do, just ask them where in the Bible they find that information—and, of course, they will not be able to tell you. So go through the Ten Commandments with them to show what the Bible really says about God's standard of goodness.

4. What if you are wrong?

On one of my many flights, I had an open seat next to me, but a man was sitting in the next seat over. I was writing a talk, but I would occasionally glance over to see what he was doing. He was taking notes from an article he was reading titled "Spirituality in the Neighborhood." I was curious; what was that about? There were pictures of Buddha statues throughout the article. I knew that when we got around to talking, it would be very interesting!

He took a nap, but after he woke up, we got into a conversation. He told me that he was a Unitarian Universalist minister, and that in his congregation were Jews, Christians, Buddhists, atheists, etc. He has a little bit of everything in his church. When I asked him, "When you die, what do you think is on the other side?" he replied, "I really don't know." He must be a great shepherd of his flock if he doesn't even know this answer!

He said he was hoping in reincarnation, but that people could believe anything they wanted to. His church was into social justice by doing good things for others, so they thought that whatever happens on the other side, it will be okay.

I challenged him with this question: "Is it possible that a person could believe something is going to be on the other side after death, but when he dies he finds that what he thought was going to be there was actually not there?"

He answered, "Of course."

"You are right," I said. "If someone believes there is nothing when he dies and there is something, then he is 100-percent wrong. But you can't have a wrong answer unless there is a what?"

He looked at me and gulped; he knew I had him. He replied, "A right answer."

"Exactly. There has to be a right answer for eternity, and you just said so. That means there is eternal truth. That being the case, then the people in your congregation have wrong answers for eternity. What are you going to do about it?"

With a not-so-friendly look on his face he said, "I really don't like the terminology that we are using right now."

That was no surprise! He had just been forced to admit that there were right and wrong answers, yet he doesn't believe in right or wrong. This is a great argument to use with people. Either there is something when we die or there is nothing. We can't all be right when it comes to our opinions on eternity. If there can be a wrong answer for eternity, then there has to be a right one. And we must let people know what that one right answer is!

This is also a great question to ask at the end of a conversation to get someone to think about the eternal consequences of his decisions. But be prepared: you can expect the person to send this question right back in your direction. How would you answer if someone asked you if *you* were wrong and this whole Jesus thing wasn't true? Have you ever thought about that? You see that everyone cannot be right here. For example, Muslims do not believe that Jesus died on the cross, let alone rose from the dead, whereas Christ's death and resurrection are the whole basis for Christianity. We cannot all be right. What if *we* are wrong?

We can't all be right about eternity. If there can be a wrong answer for eternity, then there has to be a right one.

Many Christians would answer the question by saying that they would just die and go to their grave if it wasn't true, so they have nothing to lose. But that cannot be the whole answer to the question. One guy told me, "You have believed in the Easter Bunny and Santa Claus. At least I had fun in my life partying, and then we both go to the grave." He had a valid point. If this whole Jesus thing isn't true, we have wasted our lives. We have prayed to someone who doesn't exist. We have given people hope for eternity that isn't there. Paul said, "And if Christ be not raised, your faith is vain; ye are yet in your sins...If in this life only we have hope in Christ, we are of all men most miserable" (1 Corinthians 15:17-19).

We should be the most miserable of all people if Jesus gives us hope only in this life and not into eternity. Our faith is literally in vain if Jesus did not rise from the dead.

I answer this question by telling people that, first, I have believed in the only faith that has evidence to back it up. When you study other religions, you definitely find this to be true. Second, my life has been changed by believing in Jesus Christ. I have been on both sides of the fence, living in sin and serving Jesus. I will take this life over that other life anytime. And third, if my belief was wrong, I would die and go to my grave, and that's all there is.

Now, turn the question right back on them. After giving my answer I ask people, "If you are wrong, you are literally choosing Hell for all of eternity. Are you sure you want to do that?" Of course, the answer is always "no."

We need to get people to think about the eternal consequences of their earthly actions and decisions. The New Testament talks twice as much about Hell as it does about Heaven, so we don't need to be afraid to talk about Hell with people. As a matter of fact, the loving thing to do is to make sure that no friends of yours, and no strangers you encounter, will go to Hell when they die.

You can now see how valuable these "four deadly questions" are. Use them often as you share your faith.

And it was about the sixth hour, and there was a darkness over all the earth until the ninth hour.
Luke 23:44

Chapter 10

Good Answer!

"Do you want arguments for soul winning? Look up to Heaven, and ask yourself how sinners can ever reach those harps of gold and learn that everlasting song, unless they have someone to tell them of Jesus, who is mighty to save. But the best argument of all is to be found in the wounds of Jesus. You want to honor Him, you desire to put many crowns upon His head, and this you can best do by winning souls for Him. These are the spoils that He covets, these are the trophies for which He fights, these are the jewels that shall be His best adornment."
CHARLES HADDON SPURGEON

My former students used to call Colossians 4:2–6 the witnessing passage. It says: "Continue in prayer, and watch in the same with thanksgiving; Withal praying also for us, that God would open unto us a door of utterance, to speak the mystery of Christ, for which I am also in bonds: That I may make it manifest, as I ought to speak. Walk in wisdom toward them that are without, redeeming the time. Let your speech be alway with grace, seasoned with salt, that ye may know how ye ought to answer every man."

In this chapter we will look at "how to answer everyone"—how to gently and lovingly explain to the lost what we believe and why.

A man I was witnessing commented as I answered his questions, "You've really thought about this, haven't you?"

"Of course, I have," I replied. "My eternal destination rests upon my belief and trust in God."

What he was implying was that he had met a lot of people who say they believe in God, but who had no information to back up their belief. We should be educated believers. First Peter 3:15 tells us to "sanctify the Lord God in your hearts: and be ready always to give an answer to every man that asketh you a reason of the hope that is in you with meekness and fear." When witnessing, though, even if you answer every question, that does not mean the person will be saved that day. So don't feel pressured to have all the answers. The Spirit of God has to draw the lost to Himself; we just plant the seeds. The more we know, however, the stronger our faith becomes, and the more we can help the lost as they search for truth. So let's take a look at some of the basic questions and arguments you may encounter in witnessing.

"There is no absolute truth."
Always remember that all truth, by definition, is very narrow. It has one right answer and many wrong answers. For example, $2 + 2 = 4$, not 5, not 11, not 67 (one right answer and many wrong answers). There is only one person who is the president of the United States right now (one right answer and many wrong answers). I would expect when it comes to eternity that there would be one right answer and many wrong answers. And that is exactly the case. There is only one truth, and it's found in the Bible. We must continue to steer people toward the eternal truth of God's Word.

A great statement to use with both saved and lost people is: It doesn't matter what you believe, it matters what is true. People need to think about *truth* rather than just *belief*. I might believe that the earth is flat, but it isn't. I might believe the sky is green, but it isn't. I might believe you will send me a thousand dollars, but you probably won't! We must help people distinguish between their beliefs and what is true.

At one of my high-school reunions, we had a group photo taken. I am 6'6", so as you might guess, I am always in the back row of photos.

This time, not only was I in the back row, but I was placed on a chair in the back row! One thing to look for in witnessing is a captive audience. The guy next to me, Jim, wasn't going to be going anywhere for a while, so I decided to have a conversation with him.

He'd been a popular football player in high school. His Rolex watch and large gold ring said he was fairly successful. I asked Jim what was happening spiritually in his life.

We must help people begin to distinguish the difference between what they believe and what is true.

In explaining his spiritual beliefs, he said that, as long as he believed in his heart that something was true, then it was true. One issue you'll encounter frequently when witnessing is the concept of absolute truth versus relative truth. The belief that truth is relative to a given situation.

Here is one of the arguments that I use: "Adolph Hitler killed six million of God's chosen people. So as long as he believed in his heart that it was an okay thing to do, then it was definitely okay to do, wasn't it, Jim?"

At this point Jim is in a bind. I have had only three people answer yes to that question. Some people get caught in their argument and don't want to admit that they are wrong.

Jim answered, "There must be some absolute truth." Then he turned and looked away.

Never end a conversation about Jesus on a negative note; He is way too important for that.

So I added, "Jim, if you ever want to find absolute truth, you can find it in the Bible." I could see in his eyes that a good seed had been planted.

One night after witnessing, I watched "Politically Incorrect." The purpose of the show is simply to have guests share their opinions for thirty minutes. This night there was a very conservative woman on the show who did an excellent job of stumping the others. One question she asked was, "In what situation is rape okay?" The other guests just sat there.

Think about it. Can you think of one situation in which it would be okay? Since it is wrong for all people, in all places, at all times, then the statement "rape is wrong" would be an absolute truth. And if there is one absolute truth, there can be two, three, or more. That is a great argument to help people reason it out and conclude that there must be absolute truth. You are then well on your way to being able to prove your position on the truth of God and the Scriptures.

"Can you prove that there is a God?"
People frequently ask this question, implying that our faith is blind while reason is on their side. In other words, we have blind faith, but they have calculated faith. I completely disagree with their assessment. God has never asked us to have blind faith, and He never will. Blind faith is what leads people into cults. We use calculated faith for most decisions in life, and we should do the same for eternal decisions.

Proving to the lost that there is a God is not difficult, especially since Romans 1:19 tells us that "that which may be known of God is manifest in them; for God hath showed it unto them." One of the basic proofs for God has four points:
1) Creation
2) Design

Good Answer!

3) Art
4) Order

I was at Louisiana State University in Baton Rouge one day and chatted with a theater professor as he was walking to class. He asked, "Can you prove there is a God?"

I said, "Sure, I can."

By the way, a good question to ask an atheist or agnostic is, "What evidence have you found that proves to you that there isn't a God?" Atheists never have an answer to that, and many have admitted that they have no evidence to prove their belief. Therefore, what they have is blind faith. What they mistakenly accuse us of having is actually what they are using as the basis for their eternal destiny.

I explained to the professor as we walked, "Every time you see a shirt [name an item around you], you know it has a creator. Every time you see a watch, you know it has a designer. Every time you see art [point out something artistic around you], you know there is an artist. Every time you see order, like twenty Coke cups in a row, you know there is an orderer.

"When you look around the universe, what do you see? You see creation, design, art, and order. If every other thing has a creator, a designer, an artist, and an orderer behind it, why would you not think that there is a Creator, a Designer, an Artist, and an Orderer behind this universe?"

He was silent for a minute as we walked along; he could not refute the obvious. We kept talking. Ten minutes later as we approached his classroom, he said, "I am still thinking about that creation, design, art, order thing." It was so simple and logical, yet it touched his heart.

Romans 1:20 says, "For the invisible things of him from the creation of the world are clearly seen, being understood by the things that are made, even his eternal power and

Godhead; so that they are without excuse...." People will have no excuse before God if they claim there wasn't enough evidence for Him, because the creation speaks of a Creator. How do we know a building had a builder? Just by looking! The building itself is the proof that there is a builder. This universe itself is the proof that there is a God. Period.

How do you know the Bible is true?
This is probably the most frequent question you will encounter. People want to know, as Pilate did, "What is truth?" (John 18:38). In John 17:17, Jesus says of God's Word, "thy word is truth." Definitely, all of the Bible's internal information points to it being the true Word of God.

However, many people would accuse you of circular reasoning if you argued your case this way. Most Christians just say that they believe it to be true. But remember that it doesn't matter what you believe—it matters what is true. So is there any external evidence that proves the Bible is true? You'd better believe it!

I usually discuss five points to show that the Bible is true. After I shared this information at a retreat, people told me that it was one of the most valuable things they learned.

1. The Bible is the best-selling book in the world.
That alone doesn't mean that the Bible is true, but because it is the best-selling book in history, we should take a look at it. Approximately 150 million Bibles are printed per year! No other book even comes close.
If people spend time reading Shakespeare or John Grisham, why don't they read the most popular book in the world?
Challenge people with the thought that there is a good chance the Bible contains at least some truth; reading it is a great way to find out.

GOOD ANSWER!

2. The Bible claims to be written by God.
This is a crucial point. Lost people believe that man wrote the Bible, but the Bible claims that God is the author:

> All Scripture is given by inspiration of God…(2 Timothy 3:16).

> For the prophecy came not in old time by the will of man: but holy men of God spake as they were moved by the Holy Ghost (2 Peter 1:21).

However, just because the Bible claims God as its author, does that mean He is? Actually, no it doesn't. I could write you a letter telling you what to do, and sign it "Love, God." But that doesn't mean God wrote it.

We need more proof than that. One preacher stated that the Bible uses "thus saith the Lord" and similar phrases over 3,000 times. The Bible certainly claims its authorship is divine, not human.

These first two points may pique people's interest. The next three are the hard evidence for which they are looking.

3. Historical evidence supports the Bible.
No one has yet been able to identify a single historical mistake anywhere in the Bible. That in itself is amazing. If man wrote it, we would certainly find historical errors after all these years—but there are none. So that you can study more on this point, as well as on the next two, I recommend that you read any of the following books:

- *New Evidence That Demands a Verdict,* by Josh McDowell (Thomas Nelson)
- *The Case for Christ,* by Lee Strobel (Zondervan Corp.)
- *The Signature of God,* by Grant Jeffrey (Word)

All three books provide powerful evidence that the Bible is not from the hands of man, but from the hand of Almighty God. I often buy one of these books for people who are truly searching.

4. Archaeological evidence supports the Bible.

To date, archaeologists have not discovered a single thing in the Middle East that has proved the Bible wrong. As a matter of fact, each additional discovery continues to prove it true. There have been more than 25,000 archaeological finds relating to people, places, and events in the Bible, and not one has contradicted anything in the Scriptures. That's incredible proof of the Bible's trustworthiness.

> *There have been more than 25,000 archaeological finds relating to the Bible, and not one has contradicted anything in the Bible.*

The three books mentioned above contain numerous quotes and great information about this archaeological evidence, so I won't try to repeat it here.

After citing some of the archaeological evidence for the Bible, I often tell people, "If you can believe the historical and archaeological evidence for the Bible, why don't you think you can believe the spiritual part of the book?" That often gives people food for thought.

5. Fulfilled prophecies validate the Bible.

If you do not have much time in a conversation, skip the first four points and begin with this one. Fulfilled prophecies not only prove the Bible true, they also are a proof for God.

I often ask people, "What is the only book in the world that contains hundreds of very detailed prophecies?" The correct answer is the Bible. The Book of Mormon doesn't;

the Koran for Muslims doesn't; the Bhagavad Gita for Hindus doesn't.

I ask, "If the text contains prophecies that do not come true, what does that say about that book?" People will answer that the book is false. And that's absolutely right. A guy I was talking with pointed to a trash can and said, "It belongs in that trash can right there!" He knew that if a book predicted something that didn't come true, the book could not be trusted.

I point out to people that when the Bible was written, 25 percent of the content predicted future events. And every single one of those prophecies has come true in the minutest detail, except for the few remaining prophecies about the return of Jesus Christ to earth. Statistically, there is no way that man can predict the future with 100-percent accuracy. I then ask people, "Who is the only one who can do this?"

One time I asked this question of an atheist, and he answered "God"—and he doesn't even believe that there is one! But he recognized that only God could know the future.

When people admit that, you have them. You can then explain that—according to the Bible, which is true—there is a Heaven and a Hell, and ask which place they want to go to. Then discuss the Ten Commandments, repentance, and the cross to show them their need for the Savior.

Sometimes the person I'm witnessing to will ask what some of the prophecies are. I usually use the following three:

- The Book of Micah (5:2) tells us that the Messiah will be born in Bethlehem—not in Jerusalem, Atlanta, or New York. And Jesus was born in Bethlehem (Luke 2:4–7).

- The Book of Zechariah (11:12,13) says that this Messiah will be betrayed for thirty pieces of silver. Jesus was betrayed for thirty pieces of silver (Matthew 26:15).

- The Book of Psalms (chapter 22) says that this Messiah will be pierced in His hands and His feet. This prophecy is amazing because it was written 800 years before crucifixion was ever used as a means of punishment, yet Jesus was pierced in His hands and feet (Matthew 27:35).

At that point many people say, "That's enough. You really know your stuff." Do you know what, Christians? We *should* know our stuff. And when we do, the lost appreciate it. They are looking for people who have taken a calculated step of faith in Jesus, not a blind leap of faith. The Bible is true. You can prove it, so don't ever be afraid of that question.

Remember that it is not circular reasoning to cite fulfilled prophecies, or prophecies that are coming true today (such as Matthew 24 and 2 Timothy 3). The Bible is not just a single book, but a compilation of sixty-six books written by some forty authors over 1,500 years. Its internal consistency and fulfilled prophecies prove its divine origin.

"Doesn't evolution prove the Bible false?"

The good news is that a wealth of information from the scientific community disproves evolution. This is a crucial topic for many people, and is the reason many do not believe in God. The more you know on this topic, the better. I use a four-step process to show that evolution cannot be true:

1. *Probability.* Let's say you had a cup with twenty dice, each labeled with a letter of the alphabet (a, b, c, etc.), and you wanted to roll the dice and have them come out in alphabetical order. The chance of this occurring is 1 in 2.4×10^{18}! And that is for only twenty things to occur in order. We have 206 bones in our body; how long would they take to appear in order? For 200 things to occur in order, the probability is 1 in 10^{375}. Mathematicians say that anything over 10^{50} is absolutely impossible.

2. *Fossil record.* Even Darwin stated that the fossil record should contain millions of transitional forms to show that evolution is true. Interestingly, the fossil record doesn't contain a single transitional form! It contains only complete kinds, but no transitional forms.

3. *Missing links.* Every "missing link" between ape and man has now been scientifically disproved. This includes Lucy, Piltdown Man, Peking Man, Neanderthal Man, Nebraska Man, etc. Derived more from fertile imagination than from fossil evidence, all have been shown to be either fully ape or fully human.

4. *Why are there no missing links today?* We see only whole dogs, cats, horses, birds, etc. We do not see creatures that are half cow and half whale, or half dog and half cat. They just aren't there.

I discuss these in more detail when I am witnessing. I chatted with one college student who claimed that, since evolution is true, there is no God. As I went through these four points with her, she could not argue them from a scientific perspective—and her major was anthropology. She was studying evolution, but she couldn't disprove these points!

The book that had the greatest impact on me in this area is *The Collapse of Evolution,* by Dr. Scott Huse (Baker Book House). It is the source for all the preceding arguments. Remember, science is on our side. And once you've proved the Bible true, it supports your position against evolution:

> All flesh is not the same flesh: but there is one kind of flesh of men, another flesh of beasts, another of fishes, and another of birds (1 Corinthians 15:39).

> And God made the beast of the earth after his kind, and cattle after their kind, and every thing that

creepeth upon the earth after his kind: and God saw that it was good (Genesis 1:25).

"How can Jesus be the only way to God? Aren't there many paths to Heaven?"
As our society becomes more pluralistic, increasing numbers of people think all faiths are equal and that people should simply believe whatever they want to believe. Oprah Winfrey shared her beliefs one day on her show. She pictures God at the top of a mountain, and believes there are many paths to get there. We can take the Christian path, the Jewish path, the Muslim path, the Hindu path, the good-works path, etc.

When someone makes a similar claim, here is my response. If there are many paths to God, did the Son of God have to die on the cross for the sins of the world? Of course, the answer is "no." If people could have remained on the Jewish path or the good-works path and still gotten to God, then Jesus did not have to endure an excruciating death on a cross as payment for our sins. Why would He die for us if He didn't have to?

The Bible says that He did this voluntarily. If He chose to lay down His life for our sins when He didn't have to, that would make it the most senseless, idiotic act in the history of the world. But study His actions and you will see that Jesus never did anything stupid in His entire life. He was sinless and always did everything perfectly.

Why would He lead the only perfect life in the history of mankind, and then pull the bonehead move of the millennium—unless it is just as He said, that He is the only way to get to Heaven? When someone asks you why you are so sure Jesus is the only way to Heaven, you might first want to respond, "What makes you so sure that He is not?" Try to let others prove their positions. You will find out very quickly that a lot of lost people are banking on blind faith.

You can then explain that, once we repent of our sins and place our trust in Jesus, we are "born again." He comes to live inside us through His Holy Spirit, giving us absolute assurance that we now have eternal life.

Talk about the Ten Commandments, repentance, the cross, and what the shed blood of Jesus can do for them. The following verses may help you:

"Look unto me, and be ye saved, all the ends of the earth: for I am God, and there is none else" (Isaiah 45:22).

Jesus saith unto him, "I am the way, the truth, and the life: no man cometh unto the Father, but by me" (John 14:6).

For there is one God, and one mediator between God and men, the man Christ Jesus. (1 Timothy 2:5).

Neither is there salvation in any other, for there is none other name under Heaven given among men, whereby we must be saved (Acts 4:12).

Hell is a very real place, according to the Bible…We need to convince people of its reality and warn them not to go there.

"I don't believe in Hell, so there can't be one."

Remember, it doesn't matter what we believe, it matters what is true. Unbelief doesn't change reality. We may believe that poison doesn't kill, but it does. We may believe that the earth is flat, but it is not. Continue to remind people to search for truth, and not just something to believe in.

Hell is a very real place, according to the Bible. Jesus spoke of it 33 times, describing its horrors in graphic detail. It is a place of eternal, conscious torment. We need to convince people of its reality and warn them not to go there.

"The Bible says we are reincarnated when we die."

Many people today believe in reincarnation because it seems cool. Who wouldn't want a chance to start over and do it all again? However, in Hinduism, where the concept of reincarnation originates, reincarnation is not a good thing but a curse. Individuals must keep returning to life on earth until they get it right. The Bible certainly does not support reincarnation. When Jesus said we must be born again, He was referring to a spiritual, not a physical, birth.

Those who place their trust in Christ are born spiritually into God's family. Each of us, when we die, will go to one of two destinations—Heaven or Hell. We will not return to earth in another form. The Bible tells us:

> When a few years are come, then I shall go the way whence I shall not return (Job 16:22).

> ...it is appointed unto men once to die, but after this, the judgment (Hebrews 9:27).

"Can God create a rock so big that He can't lift it?"

Can God create the biggest rock in the universe? Yes, He created everything. Can God lift the biggest rock in the universe? Yes, He is all-powerful. So what is the point of the question? There really is no point. It is just one of the stump-the-Christian questions that non-believers sometimes ask.

The answer to the question is "no." It may bother some people when you say that God cannot do something, but there are actually numerous things that God can't do. He can't make a square circle. He can't create a round square. He can't lie. He can't sin. He can't not love someone. But the fact that there are things God can't do doesn't mean that He isn't all-powerful. It just means that certain things are outside of His character.

Good Answer!

"When I am old, I will get right with God."
When people make this comment, I always ask them, "Can you guarantee that you will wake up tomorrow morning?" Of course, the answer is "no." So I just say, "You shouldn't put your head on your pillow tonight unless you know for sure where you are going to spend eternity."

A youth pastor once said, "Whether you are old or young isn't determined by your age, it is determined by when you die." It is an interesting statement. If a seventeen-year-old is going to die at age seventy, he has a lot of life left; relatively speaking, he is a very young man. If a seventeen-year-old is going to die a week from now, relative to his lifespan, he is a very old man.

We think "old" people have walkers and wheelchairs, but that is not necessarily the case. You could be hanging out with "old" people right now who look quite young. It depends on when those people are going to die. Since you don't know how "old" they really are in a spiritual sense, make sure you take the time to share with everyone what they will need to know before they take their last breath.

If Satan causes all sin, and therefore all death, who should we point a finger at when someone dies?

The Bible says:

> Go to now, ye that say, "Today or to morrow we will go into such a city, and continue there a year, and buy and sell, and get gain": Whereas ye know not what shall be on the morrow. For what is your life? It is even a vapour, that appeareth for a little time, and then vanisheth away (James 4:13-14).
>
> …behold, now is the accepted time; behold, now is the day of salvation (2 Corinthians 6:2).

> Multitudes, multitudes in the valley of decision: for the day of the Lord is near in the valley of decision (Joel 3:14).

"How can there be a God when there is so much evil and suffering in the world?"

Evil doesn't prove that there is no God; it only proves that there is evil. Some argue that a loving God wouldn't allow evil, so either there is no God, or He is not loving or powerful enough to prevent it.

Love by definition demands a choice. We can choose to love our parents. We can choose to love our spouse. We can choose to love our kids. We can also choose to love God, or choose not to love God. The evil that we see around the world is because people choose not to love God and obey Him. If we truly believed that people were made in the image of God, we would not do the things that we do to other people.

Be aware that when a person mentions evil like this, it might be due to a bad experience he has had. That is also true when a person is angry toward God or church. Very often, he has been hurt somehow. Try to find out what that event was, if he is willing to share it, and then minister to him. He is questioning the love of God at this point, so show it to him.

One young lady I talked with asked me, "What kind of God would take my dad away from me when I was nineteen years old?" She had been without her father for two years.

"Let me give you something to think about," I replied. "The Bible says that all death is caused by sin, and that all sin is caused by Satan. So if Satan causes all sin, and therefore all death, who should we point a finger at when someone dies?"

We should be blaming Satan and not God. There was no death in the Garden of Eden until sin entered the picture. There is no death in Heaven because there is no sin in Heaven.

After pondering this a few minutes, this college student said, "Maybe it is time that I give God another chance in my life." Keep sharing God's truth in love, and people will listen.

"What about someone in Africa who has never heard the Gospel? Is he condemned to Hell?"

When people ask me this question, I challenge them: "If you are so concerned about the person in Africa, why don't you repent of your sin and commit your life to Jesus, then go and reach that person in Africa?"

You quickly find that the individual really doesn't care about anyone in Africa. He is just trying to stump you.

Explain to the individual that people don't go to Hell because they haven't heard of Jesus. They go to Hell because they have transgressed the Law of Almighty God, which is sin (1 John 3:4).

Titus 2:11, a very interesting verse, says, "For the grace of God that bringeth salvation hath appeared to all men…." God wants to reach each person, and is making Himself available to all.

Romans 1:20 also tells us that God's invisible attributes are clearly seen in nature, so that men are without excuse. Since His grace appears to all men, but there are some who go to Hell, the bottom line is that people are rejecting God and wanting to selfishly choose their own way in life. This question is intended to be a rabbit trail. The person asking this is trying to distract you from the truth you were discussing.

So, after addressing this question, say something like, "When that person stands in front of Jesus, he may be able to say that he has never heard about Him. But when you stand in front of God, will you be able to say that you have never heard about Jesus?" One night I asked this question of a man outside of a bar and he answered, "No, because you told me about Him tonight." Always remember to turn the question right back toward the individual.

"The church is filled with hypocrites."
I was talking with a yuppie in a mall one day who had no faith in God, but said his parents were committed believers in Jesus. He blamed all of the hypocrites for keeping him away from church. I asked him, "If I walked up to you drinking a beer and smoking a joint, and shared Jesus with you, what would you think?"

"You would be just another freak in the world."

"You are exactly right," I said. "That makes me 100-percent wrong, but that doesn't make God wrong at all."

I was trying to help him make the distinction between the actions of followers (or supposed followers) and God's character. I continued, "There are hypocrites in the mall today, and it didn't stop you from coming to the mall. There will be hypocrites in the restaurant tonight when you and your girlfriend go out to eat, and it won't stop you from going there. So why in the world would you let hypocrites stop you from finding out about the one true God who loves you unconditionally and wants to forgive all of your sins?"

He liked the answer so much that when his girlfriend walked up, he had me repeat the entire answer for her!

"There are so many religions; how do I know which is the right one?"
When you take the time to prove the Bible is true, people have evidence for the truth of the Christian faith. Use the Law, the Ten Commandments, to show people their sin, because it will carry them to the cross to show them how

only Jesus can get rid of their sin. At that point, they realize that Mohammed, Buddha, Krishna, etc., cannot help them.

Also, always talk about the *resurrection* of Jesus—the historical event that sets Him apart from any other human being. When witnessing to two twenty-five-year-old women at an arts festival, I told them that Jesus stated He is the only way to get to Heaven (John 14:6). One of the ladies replied, "That is an awfully arrogant statement to make!"

When taken at face value, it is an arrogant statement—unless of course it can be backed up. So I took the time to explain about Jesus' life, death, and resurrection. When I finished, she agreed, "If that Man rose from the dead, He can make the statement that He is the only way to Heaven!"

The resurrection substantiates the words of Jesus. The eyewitness testimony of the resurrection is very convincing evidence that must be shared with the lost.

These are just a few of the questions you will deal with when witnessing. What I have suggested are not the perfect answers, but keep studying your Bible, and ask the Lord to lead you to those answers. You will only discover what lost people are asking by talking with them. So be bold, and get out there and talk with them!

> Joseph of Arimathaea, an honourable counsellor....bought fine linen, and took him down, and wrapped him in the linen, and laid him in a sepulchre which was hewn out of a rock....
> Mark 15:43, 46

Chapter 11

A Pocket Full of Tickets

> *"If you never have sleepless hours, if you never have weeping eyes, if your hearts never swell as if they would burst, you need not anticipate that you will be called zealous. You do not know the beginning of true zeal, for the foundation of Christian zeal lies in the heart. The heart must be heavy with grief and yet must beat high with holy ardor. The heart must be vehement in desire, panting continually for God's glory, or else we shall never attain to anything like the zeal which God would have us know."*
> — CHARLES HADDON SPURGEON

Now that you have the tools you need in order to talk with anyone about Jesus, allow the following stories to continue to throw wood on the fire in your heart, so your fire for the Lord will never go out.

Now Is the Time

If you knew for sure that you would die five years from now, what would you do with those five years? Many people say they would travel, drop out of school, try thrill-seeking activities, etc.

Now let's say you knew for a fact that you would die twenty-four hours from now. What would you do with those final hours? Many people give answers like: I would not sleep, I would hug my parents, I would resolve a problem that I have with someone, I would tell a certain person that I love him/her, I would share my faith, etc.

Now, here is the tough question: Are you in your final twenty-four hours here on earth? You don't know, do you? Could those friends you need to witness to be in their final twenty-four hours? You bet. So whatever you would do in those last remaining hours, do it now. Don't die with any regrets or unfinished business. Live every day like it is your last, because one day you will be right!

A believer told me, "I need to make time for God…no, that's the wrong way to say it. It is God's time; we are the ones borrowing it to do other things." That's a powerful statement. Psalm 90:12 says, "So teach us to number our days, that we may apply our hearts unto wisdom." Time is precious, so use it wisely for the Lord.

I often tell people that God doesn't need them a year from now; He needs them right now! We serve a "right-now" God. The fact is that God doesn't need us, we need Him. But He wants to use us right now. Is He using you right now to further His kingdom? If not, ask Him to. He wants to use each believer to reach this world for His Son. In Mark 16:15 Jesus tells us, "Go ye into all the world, and preach the Gospel to every creature." "Go" means "do not stay." It means put this book down, get up, and go bring the good news of Jesus to every person you can find in our lost and dying world.

One of my mottoes is: If it doesn't matter on the day you die, it doesn't matter. Will it matter on the day you die if you made a million dollars or owned two houses or were president of the United States? No. Will it matter on the day you die if you knew the Bible better than you knew today's newspaper? Yes. Will it matter on the day you die if you prayed more than you watched television? Yes. Will it matter on the day you die if you shared your faith with lost sinners? You'd better believe it will. We must, as believers, live lives that have eternal value, not just temporary value.

In Matthew 6:19–21 Jesus tells us, "Lay not up for yourselves treasures upon earth, where moth and rust doth corrupt, and where thieves break through and steal: But lay up for yourselves treasures in Heaven, where neither moth nor rust doth corrupt, and where thieves do not break through nor steal: For where your treasure is, there will your heart be also." If we know where our heart is, we will know where our treasure is; and knowing where our treasure is will tell us where our heart is.

Jesus says, in Luke 6:45, "A good man out of the good treasure of his heart bringeth forth that which is good; and an evil man out of the evil treasure of his heart bringeth forth that which is evil: for of the abundance of the heart his mouth speaketh." We speak out of the overflow of our hearts. Why are there so many people who claim to be Christians, but who can never describe a time when they have shared their faith? Why do some Christians talk about seemingly everything else but the things of the Lord? I think the answer is simple: Jesus is not the overflow of their hearts. If you want to become a better evangelist, fall more in love with Jesus. He will be on the tip of your tongue more than you could ever imagine!

Someone once said, "It seems that nobody is telling anybody about Somebody who can save everybody!" Make sure you are not a nobody, but a somebody who tells a very lost world about Jesus, the only one who can save them.

Tickets to Heaven
If I threw a birthday party for you where every guest would receive $100,000 in cash and a Mercedes convertible, and I

One Thing You Can't Do in Heaven

gave you fifty tickets to your party, how many people would you have at your party? No doubt, you would have fifty people. In fact, if on the way to your party you realized that you had a ticket remaining in your pocket, and you saw a homeless man, you would give him your extra ticket. Isn't that similar to what God has done for us? He has given us a pocketful of tickets, and it is our job to hand out ticket after ticket to a place called Heaven. Please don't forget what I am about to say; when I speak about this at events around the country, people have quoted it to me years later.

Why do some Christians talk about seemingly everything else but the things of the Lord?

Do you realize how many Christians are going to die and stand in front of God with a pocket *full* of tickets to Heaven? You had all these tickets to Heaven. You could have given them away to anyone you wanted to, but you died with your pocket filled with tickets to Heaven. My goal is that as I am about to die, I hand my last ticket to a police officer or an ambulance driver or an emergency room doctor. And then I'll take my last breath, die, and stand in front of the throne of God with no tickets to Heaven left in my pockets.

In Revelation 2:10 the Lord Jesus tells us, "be thou faithful unto death, and I will give thee a crown of life." Will you be faithful to the point of death, to your very last breath, handing out every ticket you have to a place called Heaven? Please do it because of the love you have for Jesus.

A fraternity at Auburn University had a very interesting party. Each fraternity member was given a ticket for a drawing. Tickets would be drawn throughout the evening, and the very last ticket would be drawn at midnight. Whoever had this last ticket won two round-trip tickets to the Bahamas! It was a cool party. As it grew closer to midnight, the tension mounted, and some people were buying tickets from others to enhance their chances of winning. The problem was that the last ticket was drawn only thirty minutes before the plane left at 12:30 a.m.! (It is possible to get to the Auburn airport in time—barely.) So everyone came to the party with suitcases and duffel bags, and they lined them up along the wall. If their ticket was drawn, they'd have to run over, grab the right bag (they hoped), and make a mad dash to the airport.

Amos 4:12 says, "prepare to meet thy God...." Are you prepared to meet your God? Is your suitcase packed and ready for the journey into eternity? Christians have a ticket to get into Heaven, but we forget that there is also a reward day in Heaven for believers.

But many Christians are not living a radical sold-out life for Jesus, and will not receive all the eternal rewards that they might have. But guess what? You have friends you know are heading into eternity with an empty suitcase. You would not let them go to the Bahamas with an empty suitcase, so why let them walk off into eternity without Jesus—the only thing they'll need there!

I once asked a guy, "If a young girl was standing on a curb beside you, and she began to walk into the street when cars were coming, what would you do?"

He said, "I would reach out and pull her back, so she wouldn't get hit by a car."

Jude 23 tells us to save others "with fear, pulling them out of the fire...." If we would pull someone away from danger in an earthly sense, shouldn't we pull people away from Hell in an eternal sense?

Romans 13:11-12 says, "And that, knowing the time, that now it is high time to awake out of sleep: for now is our salvation nearer than when we believed. The night is far spent, the day is at hand: let us therefore cast off the works of darkness, and let us put on the armour of light." Time is very precious. Every single day, 150,000 souls die and enter eternity. We must use our time wisely.

John Wesley stated, "You have nothing to do but to save souls. Therefore spend and be spent in this work." Solomon, the wisest man who ever lived, said that "he that winneth souls is wise" (Proverbs 11:30). Soul winners are wise people. The Bible instructs us to pray for wisdom, and God promises to give us wisdom to reach the lost for Him. Be wise!

Follow Jesus

In his book *Finishing Strong*, Steve Farrar quotes James Crook: "A man who wants to lead an orchestra must turn his back on the crowd." Leaders turn their backs on the crowd and follow their mission no matter what the crowd thinks. As you live your life for Jesus, turn your back on trying to please the crowd; face Jesus, and please Him with every fiber of your being. That's what these faithful witnesses did, and their names will be written in the annals of history:

> Now I have given up on everything else. I have found it to be the only way to really know Christ and to experience the mighty power that brought Him back to life again, and to find out what it means to suffer and to die with Him. So, whatever it takes I will be one who lives in the fresh newness of life of those who are alive from the dead. —*Cassie Bernall*, 17, Columbine martyr

> I have no more personal friends at school. But you know what? I am not going to apologize for speaking the name of Jesus. I am not going to justify my faith to them, and I am not going to hide the light that God has put into me. If I have to sacrifice everything, I will.

> I will take it. If my friends have to become my enemies for me to be with my best friend, Jesus, then that's fine with me. —*Rachel Scott*, 17, Columbine martyr

> Father take my life, yes, my blood if Thou wilt, and consume it with Thine enveloping fire. I would not save it, for it is not mine to save. Have it, Lord, have it all. Pour out my life as an oblation for the world. Blood is the only value as it flows before Thine altar. —*Jim Elliot*, martyr (written at age 21)

As I was reading the Book of Matthew recently, I noticed something new. In Matthew 4:19, Jesus said, "Follow me, and I will make you fishers of men." The first thing Jesus told His followers is that we are going to reach the lost with the best news ever heard! He did not say that we would make a lot of money at it or have a huge church, but that we would win souls for the kingdom. I shared this thought with a friend, and he told me something he had heard: "Remember that if you are not fishing, you are not following." What a statement! How many of us claim to be followers of Jesus, but don't do anything to reach the lost for our Lord?

If you read Matthew 10, you'll find that when Jesus sent His disciples out, He didn't make it optional for His followers to share their faith. They were all called to witness about the Lord. In today's Christianity, it seems that many people have made witnessing an optional part of the faith. And that is absolutely not biblical. One of the true highlights of being a Christian is to bring the good news of Jesus to the lost.

First Kings 18:21 says, "And Elijah came unto all the people, and said, 'How long halt ye between two opinions? If the Lord be God, follow him: but if Baal, then follow him.' And the people answered him not a word."

Who are you going to follow, Jesus or Satan? Jesus wants you to forsake all and follow Him. Don't do what the people did—they answered not a word; they said nothing. However, indecision is an answer. It means that you would not be following the Lord. Please be a follower of Jesus, and remember that followers fish for men.

Your Heart's Desire

In 1 Corinthians 9:16 Paul says "though I preach the Gospel, I have nothing to glory of: for necessity is laid upon me; yea, woe is unto me, if I preach not the gospel!" Paul has seen the wonders of Almighty God. He has given his life to Him. He knows that Jesus is the only answer for this life and the next. Woe to him if he doesn't share that good news with others. Woe to each one of us, if we know that Jesus is the only answer for our friends and strangers, and yet we do not preach the Gospel to them.

When Jesus sent His disciples out, He didn't make it optional for His followers to share their faith.

While teaching at a Christian school, I tried to show the students how important it is to live a radical life for Jesus off campus. One day as the students were arriving, there were prisoners clearing weeds in front of our school. In the first period, which was my ninth-grade Bible class, the students asked if we were going to go out and witness to the prisoners.

"Of course, we are!" I replied. "Why else would God have brought them here?"

I went outside to talk with the officer in charge, to make sure it was all right for us to come out. It was a very hot day, so the students and I put together enough money to buy each man a Coke.

I told the students that, after I finished talking to the men, they should hand a tract and a Coke to each prisoner. I also asked them to give a positive touch by shaking the man's hand or patting him on the back. It went very well. The prisoners were very moved, as was the guard.

When we went back inside I told my students, "Now, if you can share your faith with a prisoner, can't you share your faith with your best friend on the soccer team?"

One student raised her hand and said, "Mr. Cahill, it is a whole lot easier to witness to a total stranger than it is to witness to your best friend."

I replied, "If God put two people in front of you—one was your best friend who didn't know Jesus and the other was a total stranger—and He told you that you could take only one of them to Heaven with you, which one would you take?" Naturally, she said her best friend.

I told her, "Go and do something about it." God gives us lost friends for a reason—so we can help lead them to the Savior. Don't assume that it is easier to talk with one person over another. It is just not true.

Second Peter 3:9 says "The Lord is not slack concerning his promise, as some men count slackness; but is longsuffering to us-ward, not willing that any should perish, but that all should come to repentance." God does not want one soul to die and go to Hell. Do you have the same mindset? Ask God to give you a heart that beats for all the lost people on this planet.

The apostle Paul says in Romans 10:1, "Brethren, my heart's desire and prayer to God for Israel is, that they might be saved." Please make it your desire that your friends and your country become saved and sold out for Jesus.

In Romans 9:1–5, Paul talks of "great heaviness and continual sorrow in my heart" for the lost. Look at what Paul would give up to see his friends saved: "For I could wish that myself were accursed from Christ for my brethren..." (verse 3).

Do you realize what he was saying? Paul would literally give up his relationship with Jesus Christ, if he could, so his Jewish friends could know Jesus.

That is an amazing statement! After Paul's conversion (Acts 9), he lives for only one thing: Jesus. How could it even cross his mind to give up his relationship with his Lord? Paul loved his friends so much that he would do anything to see them living for Christ and going to Heaven.

Do you love your friends so much that you would literally do anything to see them saved? What is the craziest thing you would do to help someone get saved? Would you talk with the lost? Would you do the hula-hoop ten times? Would you give $10 a week? Would you empty your bank account?

In Luke 14:33, Jesus says that "whosoever he be of you that forsaketh not all that he hath, he cannot be my disciple." Are you forsaking all for Jesus Christ? What are you holding back that you need to give to Him?

Whom Do You Love?

In Matthew 7:20, Jesus says "by their fruits ye shall know them." Your works will show if you know Jesus. Titus 1:16 says, "They profess that they know God; but in works they deny him, being abominable, and disobedient, and unto every good work reprobate." Whether you love Jesus or Satan will be evident by how you spend your time and resources. Do your Friday and Saturday nights show that you love Jesus or that you love Satan? Whom do your works show that you love?

Why do people spend money on their kids? Simply because they love them. Do you spend a good deal of money on the things of God? If you do, it is probably because you love Him so much. If you don't, it might be because you don't love Him half as much as you think you do. Take a look

A Pocket Full of Tickets

at your checkbook and your credit-card statements. That's a simple way to find out who or what you love the most. Remember that God wants our first fruits, not our last fruits.

First Corinthians 3:11–15 lets us know that all of our works will be tested by fire. Any gold, silver, or precious stones will be refined by that fire and become more precious. Any wood, hay, or straw will turn to ashes in the fire.

Leonard Ravenhill advised an evangelist, "Make sure when you die that you are not standing knee-deep in ashes." In other words, make sure your works will last for eternity. Are your actions today valuable in a temporary sense or in an eternal sense? Make sure you are doing things for the Lord that will have value for all of eternity.

> *"Make sure when you die that you are not standing knee-deep in ashes." In other words, make sure your works will last for eternity.*

In his book *Finishing Strong*, Steve Farrar wrote:

> Vision will enable you to keep daily focus.
> Vision will enable you to be faithful each day.
> Vision will enable you to fix your eyes on Jesus.
>
> If you could go back in a time machine, two thousand years ago, to the times of the New Testament, it might give you some perspective.
>
> If you were to plant yourself in a busy market near the temple in Jerusalem, you could gather some real insight.
>
> Stop and think what it would be like to randomly interview the citizens of Jerusalem as they went about their daily business in the times of the early church.
>
> You would only need to ask a couple of questions.
>
> "Who do you think that people two thousand years from now will remember from your generation?"

My guess is, many of those citizens of the Roman Empire would answer, "Caesar." Others would respond, "Nero."

"But what about this group of people known as Christians? Don't you think that anyone will remember them or their leaders?"

"Are you kidding? That group of nobodies? They don't have any influence. They aren't important."

"You mean you haven't heard of Paul or Peter? Don't you think they'll be remembered? Or what about Mary and Martha? Wasn't their brother involved in some miracle?"

"I'm telling you, these people are insignificant. The only thing I ever hear of their leaders is that they're always winding up in jail. Trust me, in two thousand years, nobody will give them a thought."

So here we are, two thousand years later. And isn't it interesting that we name our children Peter and Paul, Mary and Martha?

And we name our dogs Caesar and Nero.

You are doing something very significant, my friend.

And He sees it.

No wonder you're going to finish strong.

When you are witnessing, you are doing things that have eternal value. Your Father in Heaven sees it. Don't stop until you see Him face to face!

Now in the place where he was crucified there was a garden; and in the garden a new sepulchre....There laid they Jesus.
John 19:41-42

CHAPTER 12

IS THERE NOT A CAUSE?

"The saving of souls, if a man has once gained love to perishing sinners and his blessed Master, will be an all-absorbing passion to him. It will so carry him away, that he will almost forget himself in the saving of others. He will be like the brave fireman, who cares not for the scorch or the heat, so that he may rescue the poor creature on whom true humanity has set his heart."
CHARLES HADDON SPURGEON

King Solomon prayed "that [God] maintain the cause of his servant, and the cause of his people Israel at all times, as the matter shall require" (1 Kings 8:59). What was that cause? "That all the people of the earth may know that the Lord is God, and that there is none else" (verse 60).

What a great cause! By the way, is there not a cause that you can give your whole life to? Surrendering your entire life to Jesus will give you a passion for Him and for the lost that is indescribable.

Is that a cause that's worth dying for? It should be. Paul says, in 1 Corinthians 15:31, "I protest by your rejoicing which I have in Christ Jesus our Lord, I die daily." Paul would literally die to himself (to his selfish desires) each day and let Christ live through him. That is how he was later able to die for Jesus. Do the same. If a cause is not worth living for, it is not worth dying for. And if it is not worth dying for, it is definitely not worth living for!

John Wesley stated, "Receive every inward and outward trouble, every disappointment, pain, uneasiness, temptation, darkness and desolation with both hands, as to a true opportunity and blessed occasion of dying to self and entering into a fuller fellowship with thy self-denying suffering Savior."

Compelled by Love

What comes to mind when the word "tragedy" is mentioned: an earthquake, car accident, war, September 11th? A tragedy is knowing that someone will be dying and going to Hell for eternity, and not caring enough to do anything about it.

A tragedy is knowing someone will be dying and going to Hell for eternity, and not caring enough to do anything about it.

One day as I was driving, I noticed a woman crossing the road in front of me. Her friends on the other side of the street were waving for her to come and catch the bus. As she darted across the road, a vehicle hit her. I pulled my car over to see what I could do. Others were already gathered around to help her. I laid my hands on her and prayed that she would not die if she did not know Jesus. Someone had called 911, and an ambulance arrived very quickly.

As I drove away, a thought occurred to me. When the woman was injured, men ran over to her. Women ran over to her. White people and black people ran over to her. Nothing else mattered; someone was hurt and possibly dying, so everyone ran over to see what they could do.

You know people who are dying, who are heading into eternal flames, condemned for eternity. Shouldn't you be running to them to see what you can do for them? You know people will die; you just don't know when. Run over and talk with them—now!

Second Corinthians 5:14-15 says, "For the love of Christ constraineth us because we thus judge, that if one died for all, then were all dead: And that He died for all, that they which live should not henceforth live unto themselves, but unto Him which died for them and rose again." Does the love of Christ compel you to live a holy life? Does the love of Christ compel you to share your faith boldly? What does the love of Christ compel you to do for Him?

The prophet Jeremiah records his struggle to speak out for God:

> For since I spake, I cried out; I cried violence and spoil because the word of the Lord was made a reproach unto me, and a derision, daily. Then I said, "I will not make mention of Him, nor speak any more in His name." But His word was in mine heart as a burning fire shut up in my bones, and I was weary with forbearing, and I could not stay. (Jeremiah 20:8-9)

Is your love for Jesus burning so much in your heart that you just can't wait to tell someone about Him today?

John Wesley pleaded for such bold witnesses: "Give me one hundred preachers who fear nothing but sin and desire nothing but God, and I care not a straw whether they be clergymen or laymen, such alone will shake the gates of Hell and set up the kingdom of God upon the earth."

Wesley would tell his evangelist trainees that when they preached, people should get angry or get converted. Their message wasn't "Jesus loves you," but a biblical message of sin, righteousness, Law, judgment, and Hell. He knew *that* message would lead people to the cross and to the Savior.

Is There Not a Cause?

By the way, when you finish speaking to people, do they say, "What a wonderful speaker," or do they say, "What a wonderful Savior"?

Through Many Tribulations

In Acts 14:21-22, Luke records, "And when they had preached the Gospel to that city, and had taught many, they returned again to Lystra, and to Iconium, and Antioch, confirming the souls of the disciples, and exhorting them to continue in the faith, and that we must through much tribulation enter into the kingdom of God." Trials and tribulations follow believers who boldly stand for Jesus.

One time I was ordered to leave a mall for talking with people about Jesus. That doesn't sound American, does it? So I located a Christian law firm to help me stand up for my rights, and the case wound up going to court. The other side spent over $100,000 to keep Christians out of the mall. Isn't it amazing that the malls want our money, but they don't want our Jesus!

Some of my students who went witnessing with me had to provide depositions for the case. A week later, I went in to give my deposition. During a break, I began to witness to the court reporter who writes down all that is said. She was a very strong believer, and was glad that I was witnessing to her. She said she couldn't believe the boldness and love of my students. One of them had actually done a witnessing role-play with the opposing lawyer. The reporter said that the lawyer tries to intimidate people, but the teens' sweet spirit took him aback and he wasn't able to draw them into an argumentative conversation. She even used the teens as an example in her Sunday school lesson that week! That court case cost me nothing. The law firm I used is supported by donations. They call themselves legal missionaries, who want to keep the doors open for Christians to share the Gospel and reach the lost. If you have any questions about what you can or cannot do when it comes to witnessing in school, at sporting events, in malls, on streets, etc., give this organization a call. They would love to help you: Christian Law Association, 727-399-8300, www.christianlaw.org.

Second Timothy 3:12 assures us, "Yea, and all that will live godly in Christ Jesus shall suffer persecution." Are you facing any persecution because of your stance for Jesus Christ? If not, why not? Is it possible that you may not be living godly and boldly for the Lord Jesus? Persecution comes with the territory when we make a stand for Christ. Please know also that Jesus will see you through when those times of persecution come. For example, the Lord spoke to Paul in a vision, "Be not afraid, but speak, and hold not thy peace: For I am with thee, and no man shall set on thee to hurt thee: for I have much people in this city" (Acts 18:9-10). To remind yourself that the God of this universe will protect you at all times, especially when you are witnessing, meditate on Psalm 91.

A youth pastor in Atlanta once asked me, "Mark, why is it that when we are in church or in a good worship time, God is so big and Satan is so small; but when we go out witnessing, Satan is so big and God seems so small?"

I didn't have an answer.

He asked, "Did God change?"

"Of course not."

"That's right," he said. "God hasn't changed, but our perception of God has."

That is an incredible truth. God is big wherever you go. Whether you witness in the bar section of town, at a music festival, or during spring break, don't ever forget how big your God is!

Is There Not a Cause?

Our heavenly Father promises, "There shall not any man be able to stand before thee all the days of thy life: as I was with Moses, so I will be with thee: I will not fail thee, nor forsake thee" (Joshua 1:5).

In verse 9 He says, "Have not I commanded thee? Be strong and of a good courage; be not afraid, neither be thou dismayed: for the Lord thy God is with thee whithersoever thou goest." Trust in the Lord. When you witness and make a stand for Him, He will be with you in ways you can't even imagine.

Isaiah 30:20-21 says, "And though the Lord give you the bread of adversity, and the water of affliction, yet shall not thy teachers be removed into a corner any more, but thine eyes shall see thy teachers: And thine ears shall hear a word behind thee, saying, 'This is the way, walk ye in it,' when ye turn to the right hand, and when ye turn to the left."

You have a divine task to accomplish in this life, and God will give you the divine means to get it done!

Pray when witnessing that the Lord will lead you to the right or to the left. He will guide you where He wants you to go, and you don't have to worry about the enemy when God is in control.

During a battle in World War II, General Douglas MacArthur said, "The enemy is in front of us. The enemy is behind us. The enemy is to the right and to the left. They can't get away this time!"

Make sure that you have the same mindset.

As Steve Farrar wrote in *Finishing Strong*, "No one is without a divinely appointed task, and the divine means for getting it done." You have a divine task to accomplish in this life, and God will give you the divine means to complete it!

Enlightening the Lost

Many times as I witness, people say that they've had a conversation about Jesus before, but that this is the most interesting and intellectual conversation they have ever had on the subject. People are looking for a good, solid conversation on eternal truth. Have that talk with someone today.

At Emory University, I had been witnessing to a college student for almost thirty minutes before she asked me if I knew what time it was. I told her the time, then asked, "You're not late for class, are you?"

When she said she was, I apologized, but she replied, "That's okay; this was much more enlightening!" Eternal truth, shared in love, is very enlightening to the lost. Make sure you spend time enlightening lost people.

While I was witnessing to two guys at a big rock festival, one looked at his watch and realized that it was twenty-five minutes after the start of their favorite band. One guy said, "You don't know how much I love this band; they're why I came tonight. But what you are talking about is much more important than that band on stage!" He added that this must be a divine appointment.

He also said, "You look me in the eyes when you talk to me. I like that. That shows me that you believe what you're talking about." Look people in the eyes when you witness. You will learn a lot from their eyes, but they will learn whether you really believe what you say by looking at yours.

One time while I was witnessing, a guy kept giving me all the right answers, but something just didn't seem right. So I got more specific about sin and talked about breaking the Commandments of God. Suddenly he confessed that he had recently been arrested for the largest drug bust in the history of the county! When witnessing, watch the people as you talk. Their facial expressions, eyes, and body language can tell you a lot about what might be going on. As we continued the conversation, it became apparent to both of us that he could give me the right answers because he had grown up in church, but he had yet to surrender his life to Jesus.

Keep in mind that when you witness, you will occasionally be talking with a Christian. That is not a bad thing. Some people get frustrated because they only want to talk with lost people. But remember that there is probably a good reason the Lord has sent you there. Go through the Ten Commandments with the person. I have had many people say they were Christians, then admit that they are liars, thieves, blasphemers, adulterers, and murderers. When I ask whether they would be guilty or not guilty on Judgment Day, many have said "guilty." Then I ask if that meant they would go to Heaven or Hell. Countless people have said "Hell." At that point you know you are not talking with a Christian. These are the basics of salvation, and they don't even know them.

If people know that they are saved by the blood of Jesus, follow up with a couple more questions. Ask them, "Do you live out your faith?" Many people will tell you "no." Find out what they might be struggling with and minister to them.

Then ask, "Do you share your faith?" After I asked this question of a man on the phone, there was a five-second silence before he responded. He didn't want to answer.

Ask people if they have any friends who are dying and going to Hell. They always say "yes." Then inquire, "What are you going to do about it?" Go for their heart. It ought to bother people that they have friends who will die and go to Hell, and they're not motivated to do anything about it.

Many times I ask, "What can I do to encourage you to share your faith?" Often believers will reply, "Just your being out here has encouraged me a lot." Your boldness will challenge others to be bold. People may ask you to pray for them to be a better witness; go ahead and do it right there! It means so much to them. I have prayed with Christians for boldness in the middle of music festivals, and their eyes just light up!

I saw one of my students at a large pagan music festival. He had been waiting for two hours to meet some friends that he had lost. He said, "Mr. Cahill, there is no reason for me to be here." The place was just sin city.

"Luke," I said, "you are correct. You don't belong here as a believer in Jesus Christ. Nothing in this place is glorifying Him. Of course, Luke, you would belong here for one reason."

He looked at me and said, "If I was standing up and sharing my faith in Jesus Christ."

"Exactly," I replied. Why do you spend time at places that do not glorify the Lord? Hang out at those places with a purpose: to share your faith while you are there.

Divine Appointments

State fairs are great places to witness. One night I was talking with a young man who told me that the previous night he had been suicidal. He called a girl to talk, and told her that he was going to kill himself. She said she didn't believe him, so they talked a bit and hung up.

A little later, he put a loaded .357 Magnum to his head and pulled the trigger. The gun didn't fire. He got a dud. Suddenly the girl he had called came running into his house and slapped the gun out of his hand. As we talked, he told me his story. He was having a tough time in life. He asked, "What has God ever done for me?"

I said very excitedly, "What has God ever done for you? How about last night when He didn't allow that gun to go off, then within twenty-four hours He drew the two of us together to let you know exactly what will be waiting for you when you die? That is what He has done for you!" He really thought about that.

God is working very hard in many people's lives, but so often they don't see that it is God doing the work. I believe He will send us across people's paths to show them His hand working in their lives.

While witnessing at a music festival, I talked with a couple of teenage girls. As I was explaining the cross and what Jesus did for them, I said that the blood of Jesus can wash them as pure and as white as snow (Psalm 51:7). I then stated that people in Heaven will have beautiful white robes of righteousness signifying the purity of what Jesus had done for them (Revelation 6:11). I could see one girl's eyes light up.

She explained, "The other night I had a dream, and I saw people in Heaven. They were all walking around in beautiful robes."

"What color were the robes?" I asked her.

As tears began to well up in her eyes, she smiled and said, "White!"

She had this dream, but didn't understand the meaning of the white robes. Just a few days later, in the middle of a music festival, she had her answer! God is working on so many hearts. He will often use your voice or a tract you distribute as a way to confirm the work He has been doing with that person.

I was at a mall in Atlanta that wasn't very busy, so I struck up a conversation with a college guy selling cell phones at a kiosk. After we talked for about forty minutes, he asked me what sales classes I had taken. I told him, "None."

"No, really," he replied, "what classes have you taken?"

"I haven't taken any sales classes."

Surprised, he said, "You have used every sales technique that I use to sell a phone. Matter of fact, if anyone walks up here with even a little interest in buying a cell phone, I'll be able to make a sale."

All I was doing was presenting the eternal truth of sin and the Gospel. I added, "Oh, by the way, you may sell a cell phone, but my product is much better than what you've got!" He smiled.

He wanted more information on the truth of the Bible, so I drove home to get a book, then returned to the mall and gave it to him. Go the extra mile for people. They really respond to it because it shows your total commitment to God.

Two years later, at a different mall, I was chatting with someone as the mall was about to close. I looked down the hall and saw a guy leaning against the railing staring at me. When I finished my conversation about fifteen minutes later, he was still there so I approached him. He asked, "Do you remember me?" It was the cell phone guy from two years earlier! We were able to continue our conversation, and we had a great talk. The Lord will give you the most special divine appointments. Pray for those!

Since modern technology makes some things so much easier, I decided to make a purchase through the Internet. Of course, I couldn't get it to work correctly, so I called the number on the web site. (Couldn't I have done this from the start?) After the salesperson helped me, I said, "Can I ask you an interesting question?"

She said, "Sure."

"When you die, what do you think is on the other side?"

She told me that she'd been raised Catholic, but had no real belief right now. Her boyfriend was Buddhist, some of her friends had died recently, and so on. Erica and I talked for forty-five minutes. Finally she said, "I have had people witness to me before. They would just tell me that if I didn't accept Jesus, I would die and go to Hell. You explained why

Is There Not a Cause?

I needed Him. This has been the most interesting and informative conversation I've ever had on this subject."

I couldn't finish my Internet order yet because I had an appointment to have my wisdom teeth taken out. After my appointment, I decided to get on the Internet, finish my purchase, and do what I could to help the economy. As you might have guessed, I couldn't get it to work again. (I was wondering if I was just a fool, but I found out later that there was a problem with the site.) I looked at that phone number on the screen once again. I said, "Lord, You want me to call that phone number again, don't You?"

"We are inviting you to Heaven. It's up to you to decide what you want to do with the invitation."

My teeth were killing me, and I didn't want to talk with anyone! But because I wanted to make that purchase, I called the number. This time a different salesperson helped me. I asked her the same question: "When you die, what do you think is on the other side?"

She said, "It's very interesting that you asked me that question. I am Catholic, but my college roommate is Baptist. I have been visiting her church, and yesterday I felt a tug on my heart to go forward and give my life to Jesus. Do you think I should do this?"

God is just way too good to us sometimes! As we finished talking she said, "Do you think it is possible that God had you call tonight, so that we could have this conversation?" What do you think my answer was? We serve a great God. Keep serving Him!

My parents' next-door neighbor was having a few of her trees cut down. I started a conversation with some of the workers. One of them, a seventeen-year-old, said, "Last year, my girlfriend and I were vacationing down in Florida. Life wasn't too good, so I began to pray. I said, 'God, if You're real, show me.' And I walked out of the hotel room to find the nearest church."

He told me that when two Mormon missionaries rode up to him on bicycles, he thought they must be a sign from God. As we talked, he said, "All I am searching for is the truth." We had great conversations over the next two days. People all around us are searching for the truth. Why don't you boldly share it with them?

While a friend and I were at a restaurant, we were chatting with a waitress who told us a lot about herself. She'd had a tough family life growing up in New York. Her dad was raised Catholic, but became a Christian just a few years ago.

I asked how her relationship with her father has been since he became a Christian. Jill smiled and said, "It is like getting to know a whole new person!" Her father had completely changed, and she really loved him now. So we took time to witness to her about sin, repentance, and Jesus.

I then asked Jill, in her three years of waitressing, how many Christians had taken the time to share with her about the Lord. What do you think her answer was? Sadly, she said, "None." That is pretty dismal when you consider how many Christians she must have served during the years.

But that is what often happens in life. We compartmentalize our Christianity to just certain times in our lives, instead of letting it infuse every moment of every day. I explained to her, "We are inviting you to Heaven. It's up to you to decide what you want to do with the invitation. You can take it and throw it in the trash can; or you can take it and cash it in, and come to a place called Heaven."

I gave her some money to buy a book that I wanted her to get, then we gave her a nice tip and left. While we were talking in the parking lot, the front door of the restaurant swung open and Jill came walking out. She said with a big smile, "Mark, I am going to cash that invitation in. You will see me in Heaven one day!" She then turned and walked back into the restaurant. There are divine appointments all over the place. Just step out in faith, and watch God show them to you!

One time at a music festival, I talked with a couple about sin and the Gospel, and they both committed their lives to Jesus. They already had Bibles, and they lived right next to a church where they could begin attending. The young man told me, "A couple of days ago I prayed and asked God, if this whole thing was real, to send someone to let me know that." He pointed to me and said, "And two days later, God sends you into my life!" When you step out and share your faith, you might just be the answer to someone's prayer.

Jesus said to His disciples in Matthew 9:37-38, "The harvest truly is plenteous, but the labourers are few; Pray ye therefore the Lord of the harvest, that He will send forth labourers into His harvest." Remember that it is *His* harvest. Are you praying for others to be out there witnessing to bring in the harvest? Do you realize that someone might be praying for you to be out witnessing to bring in that same harvest? A. W. Pink said, "It is true that [many] are praying for worldwide revival. But it would be more timely, and more scriptural, for prayer to be made to the Lord of the harvest, that He would raise up and thrust forth laborers who would fearlessly and faithfully preach those truths which are calculated to bring about a revival."

A Potential Paul
The bar section of any town always draws interesting people. I was hanging out one night in the bar area of Denver, and

I walked up to three folks to get into a conversation. One of the guys wanted me to go into a liquor store to buy them some liquor.

That wasn't going to happen, so he and the girl went looking for someone to help them. But one guy stayed because he wanted to talk with me. During the conversation, I asked him if he had ever sinned. He told me "yes," but then he said, "What do you mean by sin?"

I said, "Well, like the Ten Commandments."

"Oh, I've broken all of those."

"Have you ever killed anyone?" I asked.

Very nonchalantly he responded, "Yeah."

"Ten people?"

He replied, "I don't know how many."

He told me that he had grown up in a gang in Long Beach, California, and he truly did not know how many people he had killed. When he was fourteen years old, shooting baskets in his driveway, some gang members drove by and shot his girlfriend. She bled to death in his arms. "She was the one that I knew I was going to marry," he said. "She was the one I was going to have kids with, and she died in my arms."

Can you imagine having to go through that at fourteen years of age?

As we talked, I spent some time proving that there is a God and that the Bible is true. I kept looking at his eyes, and it seemed like nothing was connecting with him. So I recommended a book to him and gave him money to buy it.

He said, "You have given me an awful lot to think about tonight." That surprised me, because I didn't think he was listening that much. Then he added, "I am going to get this book that you want me to get. And if there is as much evidence as you say there is, I am going to commit my life to

Is There Not a Cause?

Jesus. And when I do, I am going to do like you do. I am going to walk around and tell people about it!"

You don't know God's plan for the person you're talking with. You might be speaking to a Saul that God is about to turn into a Paul. Go meet some potential Pauls today!

A couple of teenagers in Dallas wanted to go witnessing, so we went to the Galleria mall. They stayed with me for about an hour, watching what I did, then I told them they were ready to go it on their own. I gave them tracts and something to write with, and sent them off. We met a couple of hours later for dinner. As we were eating, I learned that Robby, a seventeen-year-old, led a Bible study at his public high school, where he was a senior. This amazing teen was studying Greek so he could know the New Testament just like it was written! He said, "You can lead all the Bible studies you want to. You can study all the Greek you want to. But when you share your faith with a lost person, that is when the rubber meets the road. That is when you find out what you have in Jesus Christ."

When was the last time you talked with a lost person? That is truly when you find out what you have in Jesus.

Let me ask you a question: When was the last time *your* rubber met the road? When was the last time *you* talked with a lost person? That is truly when you find out what you have in Jesus. Make sure you leave a lot of skid marks as your rubber meets the road many, many times before you hit the streets of gold in Heaven one day!

By the way, what do we have in Jesus? Psalm 31:19 says, "Oh how great is thy goodness, which thou hast laid up for them that fear thee; which thou hast wrought for them that trust in thee before the sons of men!"

The psalmist asks a good question: " What shall I render unto the Lord for all his benefits toward me?" (Psalm 116:12). What shall any of us give to the Lord for all the great things He has done for us?

Why don't we just be obedient to Him? Obedience will take you into the world of the lost to give them the one thing they are really looking for: Jesus.

If you truly want to learn how to love lost people, all you have to do is spend time with them. The more you do that, the more you will see why Jesus died for them.

What Do You See?

Phipps Plaza is a very upscale mall in Atlanta. Everything is so expensive that I can barely buy a piece of gum in that mall! I like to go there to witness because most people there have money as their god.

One day, just before Christmas, I sat down on a bench next to a twenty-four-year-old who had just graduated from the University of Georgia. As Colby and I were talking, his parents walked out of a store and stood behind him.

I was thinking, *Now what is going to happen?* He wasn't a believer in Jesus, but we were at a good point in the conversation. So I decided to keep going.

As his parents listened, they gave me a thumbs-up sign. His mom began to pray. They were evangelical Christians, and were so excited that someone was witnessing to him!

Colby said, "As I look around this mall, all I see are people shopping and getting ready for the holidays." I responded, "Colby, when I look around this mall, all I see are people dying and going to Heaven or dying and going to Hell. And until you commit your life to Jesus and He lifts that veil from your eyes, you can never see people any other way than you do."

Is There Not a Cause?

While I was talking with three guys at a festival, they asked me, "How do you see all of these people?"

I said, "I see people that God is crazy about, but they just don't know it yet."

I could tell that that statement meant something to them. People sometimes have the impression that God hates them. God wants all people to repent of their sins and trust in Jesus, but He does love them no matter what.

By the way, how do you see people? Everyone around you is either dying and going to Heaven or dying and going to Hell. That is biblically true. What do you want to do about it? Do you want to affect the eternal destination of someone's soul? God hopes that you do, because He wants to use you in the pursuit of every soul on this planet.

If you won $15 million in the lottery, would you tell anyone? When I ask people that, they always say that they would tell folks, and maybe even run up and down the street and shout about it. Guess what? I have won the lottery. I had a one-way ticket to Hell canceled by the blood of Jesus Christ.

I have won the lottery! I deserve Hell more than anyone reading this book, but I am going nowhere near it when I die because of what Jesus has done for me. Have you won the eternal lottery? If you have, make sure you shout it from every rooftop in America!

> And the angel answered and said unto the women, "Fear not ye: for I know that ye seek Jesus, which was crucified. He is not here: for he is risen, as he said. Come, see the place where the Lord lay."
>
> Matthew 28:5-6

Chapter 13

Hit List

"You cannot stop their dying, but, oh, that God might help you to stop their being damned! You cannot stop the breath from going out of their bodies, but, oh, if the gospel could but stop their souls from going down to destruction!"
CHARLES HADDON SPURGEON

This chapter contains nuggets of truth that have nailed me in the heart. They are pearls of wisdom—stories, testimonies, and verses—to spur you to think and then act. I hope you enjoy them and are challenged by them.

A Faithful Witness
Psalm 89:37 states, "It shall be established for ever as the moon, and as a faithful witness in Heaven." I was thinking about this verse one day. The moon is a faithful witness in the sky. What does the moon do? Although it does affect the tides on the planet, to most people it is primarily a hunk of rock that just reflects the sunlight. That's all. On various days it is a sliver moon, a half moon, or a full moon, but it was made to reflect the light of the sun. The creation of the moon shows that there must be a Grand Creator.

The Psalmist calls the moon a faithful witness—although it can't even speak! How can that be? How can I let the moon be more of a witness for God than I am, and I can proclaim His wonderful name! Then I realized that I need to be like the moon, to do one thing with my life and my voice: I must reflect the light of the Son. Just think—if all of us Christians spent our time reflecting the light of the Son of God, how bright would this world be? We don't want to be a sliver moon, but a full, radiant, glowing moon in the dark world in which we live. That means we must be angled just right toward the Son.

Ephesians 5:16 encourages us to be "redeeming the time, because the days are evil. " Time is very precious, and we are running out of it. Because the days are becoming more evil, we must let our light—the righteousness of Christ—shine very brightly right now. How can we do that?

Let's say you took a flashlight and turned it on outside at noon on a sunny day. How bright would that light be? Not very bright. Let's say you turned the flashlight on outside at midnight. How bright would the light be then? Much brighter. Now let's say you take your flashlight into a cave deep in the earth, where no light can penetrate. How bright would your light be? It would be very bright indeed. Matter of fact, the more darkness there is, the brighter your light will shine. Your light can shine at church, but it will shine much brighter at work or school, the mall, the beach, or the bar sections of town. Why? Because those places are very dark spiritually. Jesus says, "I am the light of the world: he that followeth me shall not walk in darkness, but shall have the light of life" (John 8:12). Take your light, which is provided by Jesus, to all the darkness that you can, and illuminate that darkness with the powerful light of Almighty God.

One very dark place in which you can shine your light is prison. Prison ministry is a lot of fun; you should try it! The first time I went into a prison with Bill Glass Prison Ministries, I was so nervous that I thought my heart was going to explode. But within thirty minutes, God was showing me amazing things. Once, in a prison in Houston, three of us went into the segregation unit. This is where prisoners are placed in cells by themselves for twenty-three hours a day, and are allowed out only one hour a day for a shower and recreation. These prisoners are like caged animals. The segregation unit houses the worst of the worst: murderers, rapists, gang members, etc.

I began a conversation with one prisoner who said he was in the Mexican Mafia (one of the toughest, meanest street gangs there is). He confided that he had decided to leave the Mexican Mafia. However, there is a penalty when a member tries to leave a street gang of that magnitude—it's called death. They will kill people who leave their gang. He was in the segregation unit because there was a threat on his life. So I asked him, "Does anybody in here want to kill you?"

He said "yes," and pointed to several cells of prisoners who wanted to kill him. Then he put his finger to his mouth and made a sound to be quiet. He pointed to the adjacent cell and whispered, "The guy in the next cell wants to kill me."

I whispered hoarsely, "The guy in the next cell wants to kill you?"

He nodded. I was wondering what I had gotten myself into! Because it was obvious that this man needed Jesus, and likely that he could be dying soon, I began to witness to him. Amazingly, this twenty-year-old prisoner, tattooed from his neck to his ankles, had all the right answers. He must have grown up in church, but he had definitely taken the wrong path in life.

Don't mistakenly think that young people in your church are going to turn out perfectly for the Lord when they reach adulthood. Satan is messing with them in a tremendous way. Please invest as much time and prayer as you can in those young folks. They are definitely worth the investment.

After I had talked with this guy, I wanted to meet the hit man in the next cell. I had never met a hit man before, so

I thought this would be interesting! In that cell was Juan, a twenty-one-year-old with a blond crew cut, who looked like a typical student on a college campus anywhere in America. I asked him, "Juan, what is the worst thing you have ever done in your life? You don't have to tell me if you don't want to." I ask that at times because some people think they have done something so bad that God cannot forgive them. That is never true—it is a lie straight from the pits of Hell, from the father of lies himself.

Juan asked, "I don't have to tell you?"

"No, you don't, if you don't want to."

He replied, "I am actually thinking about doing something worse than I have ever done before." He was probably referring to killing the guy in the next cell!

I was using an evangelistic poster to share the Gospel with the prisoners. (If you use tracts or other evangelistic tools, be sure to spend time explaining sin by going through the Ten Commandments. Make sure people really understand their depraved state before the holy, omniscient God of this universe.) When we got to the end of the poster and I asked Juan if he wanted to commit his life to Jesus Christ, he replied that he did.

Sometimes I will try to talk someone out of making a decision for Jesus. I know that may sound strange, but I am trying to make sure that I didn't talk the person into it, but that the Spirit of God drew him into this decision. With Juan, I wasn't sure if he really wanted to make this commitment. So I folded up the poster and said, "Juan, I am not sure that you are ready to surrender your whole life to Jesus Christ and follow Him."

"Let me tell you something," he responded. "I am sick and tired of my life; my life is going nowhere fast. And the only thing that is going to change my life is Jesus Christ, and

I want to accept Him right now." So I unfolded my poster, figuring that if a hit man wants to accept Christ, you let him accept Christ! We took time to pray as Juan committed his life to Jesus.

As Juan then began to speak, I interrupted him, "Juan, wait a minute—that is Romans chapter 8." As he continued talking, I said, "Juan, that is James chapter 2. How do you know all those verses?"

"I don't know," he replied. "They just keep coming to me." It was one of the wildest experiences I've ever had.

Juan then said, "You wouldn't believe what I have in my cell. I have a hit list."

I asked, "What do you mean by a hit list?"

"A list of people that the Mexican Mafia is going to kill."

"Juan, you are now a born-again believer in Jesus Christ. You no longer need that hit list, so why don't you give it to me?"

He handed me a list of over seventy names and addresses of individuals that the Mexican Mafia was planning to kill. Someone gave me an idea and I sent tract booklets to everyone on the list; they might soon be dying, so they needed the Gospel pretty quickly! Since no one wrote back to me, I am not sure what happened to any of those people.

A couple of days later as I was praying, God spoke to my heart. Very simply it seemed like He asked my spirit, "Mark, are you on Satan's hit list? Is your life so radically lived for My Son, are your prayers so fervent, and your witnessing so strong that you are on Satan's hit list?" What a convicting question.

I have the same question for you. Are you on Satan's hit list? Is your life so radically lived for Jesus that Satan can't wait to get you off this planet? Is your youth group on Satan's hit list?

Or is it one of those youth groups that is more concerned about pizza, yo-yos, and Six Flags than about whether your school is going to serve Jesus? Is your church on Satan's hit list? Or is it one of those churches that is more concerned with how the building looks and the next church program than with seeing the lost throughout your city come to know Jesus?

I have made it my goal, and I hope you will make it your goal, to get on Satan's hit list. I guarantee that if you make that your goal, you will have one crazy ride through this lifetime, but one amazing entrance into Heaven when you die.

One young man wrote to me, "Not only am I going to get on Satan's hit list, he is going to highlight my name!" That young man wants to be so radical for Jesus, and cause Satan so much trouble, that Satan will have to highlight his name on that hit list!

Make sure you live so that Satan hates that you woke up today because you are taking people off his team and putting them on God's team for all of eternity!

One day I was watching the X Games on TV. It is a variety of events for skateboarders, dirt-bike racers, etc. I noticed on one of the events that when participants reached the sixty-second time limit, they were given another fifteen seconds. What was interesting was that those last fifteen seconds were called "glory time." The participants were supposed to do their best tricks then because time was running out. I want to encourage you that, in an eternal sense, it is "glory time" for us Christians. Time is running out, and it is time for us to do our best for our Savior. He will be here soon, and we must be ready—and we must make sure that the rest of the world is ready too.

Witnessing: God loves it; Satan hates it. So do you think you should be doing it?

Planting Seeds

If you put dirt and fertilizer in a flower pot, added water and sunlight, then prayed for a sunflower to grow, would it grow? No, it would not. Why? You didn't plant a seed. Once you plant a sunflower seed, *then* a sunflower can grow. Although God could do a miracle and grow something without a seed, He has established both a seed time and a harvest time. In 1 Corinthians 3:6-7, Paul reminds us how important seeds are. Someone must plant before God can give the increase. God hears our prayers when we pray for a friend to know Jesus Christ, but I think many times He wants us to go and plant a seed in that person's life. If we would just talk with that friend about Jesus and *then* pray for him, God would have a seed that He would love to make grow.

Hearing Thanks

Do you realize that every individual you have ever witnessed to will thank you one day? Think about it. If people you witness to don't accept Jesus and wind up in Hell, will they thank you? I don't believe that you will ever hear it, but I do believe they will. Once they are in Hell and realize that it is for eternity, I believe they will say, "At least that person who witnessed to me in the mall or at school that day cared enough about my eternal destination to tell me how I could have avoided this place. I really wish I could thank him." And, of course, they will wish they had listened.

Now think about the people who end up in Heaven. Imagine someone walking up to you in Heaven saying, "Remember me? I used to work (or go to school) with you, and you witnessed to me one day. I know it seemed like I wasn't paying attention, but I was listening. Three years later, I committed my life to Jesus and lived for Him. And I really want to thank you for taking the time to share Jesus with me."

If someone said that to you in Heaven, how do you think you would feel? It would be an unbelievable feeling!

Don't spend your life going after cheap thrills, such as riding on a roller coaster with your hands up, or cheering for a touchdown at a football game. Instead, go for the eternal thrill of having people thank you for what you did to help them enter the gates of Heaven for all of eternity. Make sure you hear a whole bunch of thank-yous in Heaven because you boldly proclaimed the name of Jesus here on earth.

The Greatest Sin

One night as I was preparing to go out witnessing, I was reading my Bible and praying. As I was thinking about witnessing, it occurred to me that all the lost people need Jesus, yet sometimes I don't want to talk to them about Him. I realized that not sharing my faith was really selfish. It then hit me that there are two kinds of sin in the Bible: sins of commission and sins of omission. There are sins that we commit, and there are things that we should do, but don't. "Therefore," says, James 4:17, "to him that knoweth to do good, and doeth it not, to him it is sin."

I believe one of the greatest sins believers can commit is to not tell the unsaved about the only thing that can save them.

Something began to stir in my spirit. If all sin comes down to selfishness (having a "me first" attitude instead of putting God first), and if not sharing my faith is selfish, what bigger sin will I ever commit as a believer than not telling the lost about Jesus? We think that committing adultery or murder would be a great sin—and from the words of an all-holy God, those *are* great sins. But I believe that one of the greatest sins believers can commit is to not tell the unsaved about the only thing that can save them. Jesus said to the woman caught in adultery, "Go, and sin no more" (John 8:11). As a believer, you know how much God hates sin, so please "go, and sin no more" by making sure you tell everyone you encounter about Jesus.

Do It Today
While I was visiting friends at Auburn University, I went witnessing at a mall on Friday night then came back and went to bed. About midnight, I woke up feeling that I had not done enough witnessing, so I got dressed and went down to the bar section of town to talk with people. I saw a guy sitting on a brick wall and sat down next to him. We had a great conversation. He told me that his parents were members of Navigators, a very strong Christian group, but that he had no faith in God at all. This college senior had some great questions, but there were answers for all of his questions.

After we talked for an hour he said, "I belong to the Farmhouse fraternity here at Auburn. I have been a member of this fraternity for four years. There are evangelical Christians in my fraternity who have never taken the time that you have to share Jesus with me. Do you know what? That really stinks, doesn't it?"

I had to admit that it did.

Think about that. You could have lost people in your life right now who are wondering why you have never taken the time to share the truth with them. Don't let them wonder any longer. Have that conversation with them today.

Put Another Log on the Fire
Have you ever been to a Christian camp and gotten that "camp feeling," where you are pumped up for God, but then a month or two later you are back to normal, or down in the

dumps? I wonder why that seems to happen so often. As I was thinking and praying about that one day, I got a picture in my mind that I believe was from the Lord. It was just a simple picture of a campfire. If you stop putting wood on a campfire, what happens to the fire? It goes out. But if you put wood on it, it keeps burning. James instructs us, "But be ye doers of the word, and not hearers only, deceiving your own selves" (1:22). He then tells us "that faith without works is dead" (2:20).

> *The people who are continually fired-up for Jesus are those who are doing the work of the Lord.*

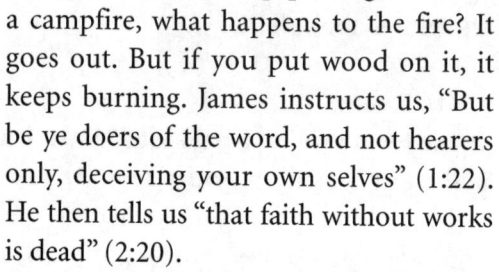

The people I meet who are continually fired-up for Jesus are those who are doing the work of the Lord. They are active in their faith: They work at homeless shelters, witness to the lost, write school papers from a Christian perspective, visit prisoners, etc. They are putting wood on their fire. And if you do this continually, not only will the fire not go out, it will grow larger. God doesn't want us to be mere campfires; He wants us to be bonfires, raging infernos for Him. Keep doing the things of God, and your passion for Him will stay strong for the rest of your life.

According to author Steve Farrar, "If you are not growing up in Christ, you are growing old in Christ."

Paul wrote (Philemon 1:6), "That the communication of thy faith may become effectual by the acknowledging of every good thing which is in you in Christ Jesus." If you want a full understanding of everything that you have in Jesus, make sure that you are active in sharing your faith.

Make Him Look Good
I heard a preacher say something that I will never forget: "We are here for two reasons: to make Him well known, and

to make Him look good." That sums up Christianity, doesn't it? We are here to tell others about Jesus, to make Him well known around the world, and to make Him look good, we are to walk like Jesus did. Do you think those two things will matter on Judgment Day? You'd better believe it! Spend your life making Him well known and making Him look good, and you will have a very satisfying life.

> "We are here for two reasons: to make Him well known, and to make Him look good."

One night in Myrtle Beach, South Carolina, I was out late witnessing to two Marines. One really wanted to talk, but the other guy kept edging away. After about ten minutes, the guy who wasn't interested wanted to leave and go smoke a joint. His buddy said, "I like talking with this guy, so let's stay."

Since they were just going up to their room, I offered to walk up there with them. As we were walking, the guy who wanted to smoke warned his friend that I might be a cop.

His buddy replied, "This guy isn't a cop. He's talking to people about Jesus!" It was pretty funny.

When we got to their room, the friendly guy said, "My buddy wants to frisk you to make sure you don't have a wire or something." So they frisked me to ensure that I didn't have a wire to tape the conversation or a gun.

I joked, "You guys watch way too much television!"

We went into their room, where they had Heineken beer on ice, and one guy began to roll a joint. As I continued talking with the other guy, he told me that one thing he liked about me was that I was dressed like they were. I was wearing black jeans and a T-shirt.

I asked him, "If I walked up to you in a three-piece suit, carrying a twenty-pound Bible, what would you do?"

He responded, "I would have nothing to do with you!"

When you're witnessing, do not wear anything that is sinful or inappropriate, but dress to fit into the place you are going to. Your countenance and your love for Jesus and for the lost should draw people to you, and not your clothes. Also, don't wear Christian T-shirts or jewelry. That can cause people to not talk with you because they know exactly where you are coming from. Jesus didn't put on anything special when He was witnessing. We should not wear things that will discourage people from talking with us or that will discredit our ministry for the Lord Jesus Christ.

I heard the guy who wasn't into the conversation call his girlfriend and tell her, "Today hasn't gone too well. This morning was terrible; this afternoon nothing good happened; and now, tonight, I have Jesus in my hotel room!"

I looked at him and said, "No, no. Not Jesus." But then it occurred to me: If people cannot see Jesus in you and me, in whom will they ever see Jesus? We must make Jesus well known and make Him look good wherever we go. I was able to give tracts to those Marines, and one of them wanted my phone number to keep in touch! We serve a great God. Keep serving Him!

Start a Revolution

The word "revolution" means a sudden, radical, or complete change; the overthrow or renunciation of one government or ruler and the substitution of another by the governed. I am not referring to Washington, D.C., but isn't it time for the overthrow of this current government? John 12:31 says, "Now shall the prince of this world be cast out." The ruler of this world, Satan, needs to be overthrown. This can be done by prayer and by Christians boldly standing for eternal truth wherever they go.

However, in order to have a revolution, you must have one thing: a revolutionary! Someone who is willing to make that stand no matter what the cost. A synonym for "revolutionary" is "radical"—someone who is giving it all that he has, pleasing God above anyone else, living for God alone. Before there can ever be a revolution in this world, there must be a revolution in you. You must make that choice to give your all to God. Would you commit to starting a revolution in this world? Many people are letting their love for Jesus cause a revolution *in* them, and it is beginning to cause a revolution *around* them. Be a revolutionary—a radical for Jesus.

Finish Strong

In 2 Timothy 4:7, Paul says, "I have fought a good fight, I have finished my course, I have kept the faith." How will you finish the race of life? It really doesn't matter how you start; what matters is how you finish the race.

Carl Lewis—the great long-jumper and sprinter who won nine Olympic gold medals—was an amazing guy to watch in the 100-meter dash. When the gun went off, you could always find Carl toward the back of the pack. He was not a good starter.

At about the 50-meter mark, Carl would near the middle of the pack. But by the end of the race, you could almost always find him at the tape in first place. Other runners said that Carl Lewis had a gear at the 60-meter mark that no other runner had. They said it was like a rocket went off in Carl, enabling him to pass everyone. The thing is, you don't win gold medals at the start, you win them at the finish.

By the way, how will you finish the race of life for Almighty God? I tell people, "You will either finish strong, or you will finish wrong." That is what Paul was talking about in this verse. He kept the faith all the way until the end of the race of life. Do the same.

One time, in a mall, I sat down near an older gentleman and began a conversation. He told me after a couple of minutes that he used to be like me, but not anymore. He had been a Disciples of Christ pastor for nine years. He said, "I used to believe what you did, but then I got educated." He told me about his five degrees from various colleges, and that he had just finished writing an article for *American Atheist* magazine.

This man is finishing the race of life very, very wrong. Make sure when you meet Jesus one day, when you cross the finish line of life and enter Heaven, that you finish the race very, very strong!

Hanging by the Fingertips

At a music festival in Nashville, Tennessee, I had a conversation with a nineteen-year-old construction worker from Detroit. He had hopped a train to Nashville to see his girlfriend. He had arrived late the night before, so I asked him where he spent the night. He answered, "On top of that building," as he pointed to a high-rise. He slept on the top of a building!

Then I asked, "What do you do for fun?"

"I'm a building jumper," he replied. I asked what that was.

"You know, like you see on TV when people jump from the top of one building to another one. It's a real rush."

I'll bet it is! Since I like to ask people questions, I asked him, "Have you ever missed?"

"Once," he said. "After I jumped from one building toward the other, as I was going through the air, I realized that I didn't have enough to get there. All I got was my fingertips over the side of the roof, and my body slammed against the side of the building. I was left hanging there. I had just enough energy to pull myself over the top."

"Were you scared?"

"Very," he responded.

Do you realize that you could be talking to people today who are hanging by their fingertips before they drop off into eternity? They could be that close. If they knew what awaited them without Jesus, they would be scared too.

In 1 Samuel 20:3, David says, "truly as the Lord liveth, and as thy soul liveth, there is but a step between me and death." Every person comes to the point where he is one step, one breath from eternity.

And we all reach the point where our own strength can't pull us out of our predicament. Tell people—as they hang on by their fingertips heading into eternity—that there is a nail-pierced hand reaching down to pull them into Heaven.

Sound the Alarm

Ezekiel 33:1–11 records the word of the LORD to the prophet Ezekiel:

> Again the word of the Lord came unto me, saying, "Son of man, speak to the children of thy people, and say unto them, 'When I bring the sword upon a land, if the people of the land take a man of their coasts, and set him for their watchman: If, when he seeth the sword come upon the land, he blow the trumpet, and warn the people; then whosoever heareth the sound of the trumpet, and taketh not warning; if the sword come, and take him away, his blood shall be upon his own head. He heard the sound of the trumpet, and took not warning; his blood shall be upon him. But he that taketh warning shall deliver his soul. But if the watchman see the sword come, and blow not the trumpet, and the people be not warned; if the sword come,

and take any person from among them, he is taken away in his iniquity; but his blood will I require at the watchman's hand.'

"So thou, O son of man, I have set thee a watchman unto the house of Israel; therefore thou shalt hear the word at my mouth, and warn them from me.

"When I say unto the wicked, 'O wicked man, thou shalt surely die'; if thou dost not speak to warn the wicked from his way, that wicked man shall die in his iniquity; but his blood will I require at thine hand.

"Nevertheless, if thou warn the wicked of his way to turn from it; if he do not turn from his way, he shall die in his iniquity; but thou hast delivered thy soul.

"Therefore, O thou son of man, speak unto the house of Israel; 'Thus ye speak, saying, "If our transgressions and our sins be upon us, and we pine away in them, how should we then live?"'

"Say unto them, 'As I live,' saith the Lord God, 'I have no pleasure in the death of the wicked; but that the wicked turn from his way and live: Turn ye, turn ye from your evil ways; for why will ye die, O house of Israel?'"

In ancient times, watchmen were positioned on the wall surrounding a city to keep watch. Their job was to be on the lookout for any armies that were coming. When they saw an enemy approaching, they were to blow the trumpet to warn the city's residents. It was not their job to make everyone ready; it was the people's own responsibility to get ready. The watchmen's job was just to sound the alarm.

God has left believers on earth to sound the alarm to others, to warn the wicked that if they do not repent of their wicked ways and come to Jesus, they will regret it both here and for eternity.

If we know the wicked are dying and going to Hell and we do not warn them, their blood is on our hands. I had enough blood on my hands when I was lost; I don't need any more. We must tell the lost about Jesus. God takes no pleasure in the death of the wicked, and neither should we. Pray for them and witness to them so that they will be in Heaven with us one day.

Earlier, the Lord told Ezekiel, "go, get thee to them of the captivity, unto the children of thy people, and speak unto them, and tell them, 'Thus saith the Lord God'; whether they will hear, or whether they will forbear" (3:11). Remember, it is our responsibility to speak the truth, whether our listeners listen or whether they refuse the message.

> *If we know the wicked are dying and going to hell and we do not warn them, their blood is on our hands.*

Be a World Changer

The Jews in Thessalonica complained about Paul and Silas, "These who have turned the world upside down have come here too" (Acts 17:6). Wouldn't it be nice to have the reputation of having turned the world upside down? We all have reputations. What is yours? Ask people you know what they think your reputation is. Ask them what they think is the most important thing in your life. It's interesting when you ask people that because, whatever it is, they will know it. If it is Jesus, others will see that. God is looking for people He can use to turn this world upside down for His Son, but His Son must be the most important thing in your life if you are to have a reputation as a world changer.

One Thing You Can't Do in Heaven

In the great Hall of Faith chapter, Hebrews 11:37-40, says:

> They were stoned, they were sawn asunder, were tempted, were slain with the sword: they wandered about in sheepskins and goatskins; being destitute, afflicted, tormented; (Of whom the world was not worthy:) they wandered in deserts, and in mountains, and in dens and caves of the earth. And these all, having obtained a good report through faith, received not the promise: God having provided some better thing for us, that they without us should not be made perfect.

I have a very simple question: Is the world worthy of you? Make sure you live a life so holy for your Lord, and so boldly reaching the lost, that this world will never be worthy of you! One of the most powerful passages of Scripture is Matthew 10:28-39. Absorb what Jesus says—and then do it:

> And fear not them which kill the body, but are not able to kill the soul: but rather fear him which is able to destroy both soul and body in Hell. Are not two sparrows sold for a farthing? and one of them shall not fall on the ground without your Father. But the very hairs of your head are all numbered. Fear ye not therefore, ye are of more value than many sparrows. Whosoever therefore shall confess me before men, him will I confess also before my Father which is in Heaven. But whosoever shall deny me before men, him will I also deny before my Father which is in Heaven. Think not that I am come to send peace on earth: I came not to send peace, but a sword. For I am come to set a man at variance against his father, and the daughter against her mother, and the daughter-in-law against her mother-in-law. And a man's foes shall be they of his own household. He that loveth father or mother more than me is not worthy of me: and he that loveth son or

daughter more than me is not worthy of me. And he that taketh not his cross, and followeth after me, is not worthy of me. He that findeth his life shall lose it: and he that loseth his life for my sake shall find it.

Fellowship of the Unashamed
(An African Martyr's Last Words)

I am part of the "Fellowship of the Unashamed." The die has been cast. I have stepped over the line. The decision has been made. I am a disciple of Jesus Christ.

I won't look back, let up, slow down, back away, or be still. My past is redeemed, my present makes sense, and my future is secure.

I'm finished and done with low living, sight walking, small planning, smooth knees, colorless dreams, tame visions, mundane talking, cheap giving, and dwarfed goals.

My pace is set, my gait is fast, my goal is Heaven, my road is narrow, my way is rough, my companions few, my Guide reliable, my mission clear.

I won't give up, back up, let up or shut up until I've preached up, prayed up, paid up, stored up, and stayed up for the cause of Christ. I must go until He returns, give until I drop, preach until all know, and work until He comes.

And when He comes to get His own, He will have no problem recognizing me. My colors will be clear. "For I am not ashamed of the Gospel of Christ" (Romans 1:16).

Be part of the Fellowship of the Unashamed. It is the only way to live this life. Remember this: To be a missionary you don't have to cross the sea, you just have to see the cross.

So then after the Lord had spoken unto them, he was received up into heaven, and sat on the right hand of God.
Mark 16:19

Chapter 14

Dear Satan or Dear God

"Lost! Lost! Lost! Better a whole world on fire than a soul lost! Better every star quenched and the skies a wreck than a single soul to be lost!"
CHARLES HADDON SPURGEON

There are only two kinds of people on earth: those who are lost and those who are saved. You fall into one of those two groups. Which one are you in? In eternity, the only thing that will matter is whether you have accepted or rejected the salvation God offers in Jesus Christ. God will not force you to accept Him. He can draw you to Him, but at some point you must surrender your life to Him.

The Ten Commandments—the Law of Almighty God—holds every one of us guilty before God because we have broken that Law. So the question is: Will you repent, turn from your sin, and surrender your life to Jesus? Read the following prayers, and decide who to follow. Whether you think you're praying or not, when you finish reading, you will be serving someone. The only question is, who?

Dear Satan, the Bible says that you are the god of this world. You are the father of lies. You deceive the nations and blind the minds of those who do not believe. God warns that I cannot enter His kingdom except by believing that Jesus died to pay for my sins. I have lied, stolen, looked with lust and therefore committed adultery in my heart. I have harbored hatred, which the Bible says is the same as murder. I have blasphemed, refused to put God first, violated the Sabbath, coveted other people's goods, dishonored my parents, and have been guilty of the sin of idolatry—I made a god to suit myself. I did all this despite the presence of my conscience. I know that it was God who gave me life. I have seen a sunrise. I have heard the sounds of nature. I have enjoyed an incredible array of pleasures, all of which came from His generous hand. I realize that if I die in my sins I will never know pleasure again. Yet today I refuse to confess and forsake my sins. On the Day of Judgment, when I am cast into the Lake of Fire, I will have no one to blame but myself. It is not God's will that I perish. He showed His love for me in the death of His Son, who came to give me life. It was you, Satan, who came to kill, steal, and destroy. You are my spiritual father. I choose to serve you and do your will because I love darkness and hate the light. If I do not come to my senses, I will be eternally yours. Amen.

Dear God, I have sinned against You by breaking Your Commandments. Despite the conscience You gave me, I have looked with lust, and thus committed adultery in my heart. I have lied, stolen, failed to love You, failed to love my neighbor as myself, and failed to keep the Sabbath holy. I have been covetous, and harbored hatred in my heart—which makes me guilty of murder in Your sight. I have used Your holy name in vain, have made a god to suit myself, and have dishonored my parents. If I stood before You in Your burning holiness on Judgment Day, if every secret sin I have committed and every idle word I have spoken came out as evidence of my crimes against You, I would be utterly guilty, and justly deserve Hell. I am unspeakably thankful that Jesus took my place in judgement by suffering and dying on the cross. He paid my fine so that I could leave the courtroom. He revealed how much You love me. I believe that He then rose from the dead, according to the Scriptures. I now confess and forsake my sin and yield myself to Jesus to be my Lord and Savior. I will no longer live for myself. I present my body, soul, and spirit to You as a living sacrifice, to serve You in the furtherance of Your kingdom. I will read Your Word daily and obey what I read. It is solely because of Calvary's cross that I will live forever. I am eternally Yours. In Jesus' name I pray. Amen.

Jesus tells us, "No man can serve two masters: for either he will hate the one, and love the other; or else he will hold to the one, and despise the other. Ye cannot serve God and mammon" (Matthew 6:24). Which master will you choose to serve for the rest of this life and for all of eternity?

Joshua 24:15 says, "And if it seem evil unto you to serve the Lord, choose you this day whom ye will serve…but as for me and my house, we will serve the Lord." Who will you choose to serve? I pray you will choose to serve the God of this universe with every fiber of your being. I really hope to see you in Heaven one day!

My hope and prayer is that you will choose to serve the God of this universe with every fiber of your being.

If you are a believer in Jesus Christ, I hope you have enjoyed this book; but more importantly, I hope that when you put it down, you will talk with a lost person about Jesus today. I will see you in Heaven one day if you are a born-again believer. And when I do, make sure you are not by yourself, but that you have a crowd of people with you! Have a blessed time sharing your faith in Jesus Christ!

"And when these things begin to come to pass, then look up, and lift up your heads; for your redemption draweth nigh." (Luke 21:28)

Mark Cahill has a business degree from Auburn University, where he was an honorable mention Academic All-American in basketball. After spending a few years in the business world, he surrendered his heart to Jesus Christ and asked God to place him where he could touch as many lives as possible. Within a year, he was teaching school. Although Mark planned to teach for the rest of his life, God moved him from teaching at a Christian high school to devoting a year to full-time evangelism. He then embarked on a speaking career. Mark speaks to over 25,000 people a year at churches, retreats, conferences, camps, etc., equipping and challenging the saved to go out and reach the lost. As one of his students noted, he's still teaching, but in a much bigger classroom.

His true vocation is witnessing, whether at malls, music and art festivals, beaches, sporting events, bar sections of towns ...wherever the lost can be found. Mark lives in Stone Mountain, Georgia.

∼

To arrange a speaking engagement, contact the **Ambassador Agency** toll-free at 877-425-4700 or www.ambassadoragency.com

To download the free Study Guide, order additional books or resources, sign up for the free e-newsletter, or donate to this ministry, go to
www.markcahill.org

Contact Mark Cahill at: P.O. Box 81, Stone Mountain, GA 30086
800-NETS-158 / 800-638-7158 • Email: mark@markcahill.org

One Heartbeat Away:
Your Journey Into Eternity

Believer or nonbeliever, if you are looking for evidence for faith, you will find it here. People of all ages continue to testify to the impact Mark's latest book has had on their lives.

One reader had this to say, "GREAT BOOK!!! The apologetics book for this decade."